How to Make Money as a Mediator (and Create Value for Everyone)

Jeffrey Krivis and Naomi Lucks

How to Make Money as a Mediator (and Create Value for Everyone)

30 Top Mediators Share Secrets to Building a Successful Practice

JOSSEY-BASS
A Wiley Imprint
www.josseybass.com

Copyright © 2006 by Jeffrey Krivis and Naomi Lucks. All rights reserved.

Published by Jossey-Bass
A Wiley Imprint
989 Market Street, San Francisco, CA 94103-1741   www.josseybass.com

No part of this publication may be reproduced, stored in a retrieval system, or transmitted in any form or by any means, electronic, mechanical, photocopying, recording, scanning, or otherwise, except as permitted under Section 107 or 108 of the 1976 United States Copyright Act, without either the prior written permission of the publisher, or authorization through payment of the appropriate per-copy fee to the Copyright Clearance Center, Inc., 222 Rosewood Drive, Danvers, MA 01923, 978-750-8400, fax 978-646-8600, or on the Web at www.copyright.com. Requests to the publisher for permission should be addressed to the Permissions Department, John Wiley & Sons, Inc., 111 River Street, Hoboken, NJ 07030, 201-748-6011, fax 201-748-6008, or online at http://www.wiley.com/go/permissions.

Limit of Liability/Disclaimer of Warranty: While the publisher and author have used their best efforts in preparing this book, they make no representations or warranties with respect to the accuracy or completeness of the contents of this book and specifically disclaim any implied warranties of merchantability or fitness for a particular purpose. No warranty may be created or extended by sales representatives or written sales materials. The advice and strategies contained herein may not be suitable for your situation. You should consult with a professional where appropriate. Neither the publisher nor author shall be liable for any loss of profit or any other commercial damages, including but not limited to special, incidental, consequential, or other damages.

Readers should be aware that Internet Web sites offered as citations and/or sources for further information may have changed or disappeared between the time this was written and when it is read.

Jossey-Bass books and products are available through most bookstores. To contact Jossey-Bass directly call our Customer Care Department within the U.S. at 800-956-7739, outside the U.S. at 317-572-3986, or fax 317-572-4002.

Jossey-Bass also publishes its books in a variety of electronic formats. Some content that appears in print may not be available in electronic books.

Library of Congress Cataloging-in-Publication Data

Krivis, Jeffrey, date.
   How to make money as a mediator (and create value for everyone) : 30 top mediators share secrets to building a successful practice / Jeffrey Krivis and Naomi Lucks.
      p. cm.
   Includes index.
   ISBN-13: 978-0-7879-8204-1 (cloth)
   ISBN-10: 0-7879-8204-0 (cloth)
   1. Mediators (Persons)—Vocational guidance. 2. Conflict management. 3. Mediation. 4. Dispute resolution (Law). I. Lucks, Naomi. II. Title.
   HD42.K756 2006
   303.6'9—dc22   2006000731

Printed in the United States of America
FIRST EDITION
HB Printing   10 9 8 7 6 5 4 3 2 1

Contents

Acknowledgments	vii
Introduction: How I Found My Dharma in Mediation	1
1. Extreme Mediation: What Top-Tier Mediators Know That You Can Learn	9
2. Be Yourself: Inspiring Trust, Projecting Authenticity, Honing Your Skills	33
3. Invisible Marketing: The Essence of Networking	53
4. Visible Marketing: Getting Out There	77
5. Practical Considerations: The Business of Mediation	109
6. How Much Money Can You Earn? Value, Investment, and Cold, Hard Cash	137
7. Staying Alive: Weathering the Ups and Downs of a Mediation Practice	157
8. Looking Ahead: The Future of Mediation and *Your* Future in Mediation	177
The Mediator's Field Guide to a Successful Practice	199
About the Authors	221
About the Contributors	223
Index	233

*To our friends and colleagues at the
International Academy of Mediators*

Acknowledgments

This book is a result of a unique collaboration with prominent practitioners who have shared their unvarnished insight into the ideas, attitudes, and approaches that have made them successful. This unique collaboration seeks the larger objective of helping our fellow mediators achieve their goals of prosperity and productivity. For this reason, the men and women who contributed to this book deserve a standing ovation: the sum total of their cumulative knowledge far exceeds what two people writing this type of work could have brought to the field.

We are truly grateful to many of our friends and colleagues at the International Academy of Mediators, who have provided unconditional access to their years and years of experience in the marketplace.

This book would not have been written without the vision and insight of Alan Rinzler of Jossey-Bass, an imprint of John Wiley & Sons. We also want to thank the rest of the staff at Jossey-Bass, including Seth Schwartz, Muna Farhat, Carol Hartland, Paula Goldstein, Brian Grimm, Karen Warner, Michele Jones, and Joanne Farness.

How to Make Money as a Mediator (and Create Value for Everyone)

Introduction
How I Found My Dharma in Mediation

When I found my dharma in mediation, everything fell into place.

Jeff Krivis

It's a given: *no one* goes into mediation to make their fortune. Virtually every successful mediator I know—whether their specialty is employment, entertainment, insurance, personal injury, family law, public policy, or something else—was drawn to the field for its richness and possibility. Each one of them thinks of mediation not just as a job but as a vocation: a calling. Many of them—including former litigators who were making a lot more money taking cases to court—stay in the field despite the fact that they are not earning anywhere near their former salaries.

Still, a small but growing number of mediators today are making a very comfortable living in the low to middle six figures, and a few are enjoying returns verging on and even achieving seven figures. How do they do it?

And how can *you* do it?

That's what this book is about. We spoke to some of the most successful mediators in the business and asked them to share their experiences, their advice, and even their secrets. And we discovered something interesting in the process: despite the fact that we all began in different fields (including corporate business, commercial litigation, teaching, insurance adjusting, and social work) and practice in different geographical areas (from California to Michigan to Hawaii, from Canada to New Zealand), we all share similar feelings about what it takes to become a successful mediator.

MY STORY

I never planned to become a mediator. When I was in law school and for the first years of my practice, mediation wasn't an option. In fact, it wasn't even a field. Then, in 1989, everything changed.

At age thirty-three, I had a successful litigation practice earning a respectable six-figure income—that was, and is, a lot of money for a young guy, and there was no monetary reason for me to change what I was doing. But when I thought about my future, I just couldn't see myself summarizing depositions and responding to interrogatories for the next thirty years.

Then a client asked me to settle a case through a mediator. A mediator? We didn't have those in California, I told him, but I knew that other states did. I looked around, asked a few questions, and eventually the client referred a mediator from Texas, Richard Falkner, to work with me. It didn't take me much time to discover that the process worked and to find that I admired its authenticity. In short, mediation felt right, and I connected to it.

When the case was settled, I asked Richard, "Do you really do this for a living?"

"Yes," he replied. "It's part of our state court system." And then a great thing happened: he invited me to go to Texas and get training in the mediation process with his partner, Gary Kirkpatrick; this personal approach was pretty much the only kind of training there was in those days. I jumped at the chance, hopped on a plane, and spent a few days attending an interactive workshop on mediation. Those few days illuminated my future, showing me a vision of what was possible and what my life could look like. I returned home inspired. I would be a mediator.

Getting Started

After I came back I investigated around the country to see who was doing this for a living. I soon discovered the Connecticut Mediation Project, which had been started by the state's insurance industry to get trial lawyers to come to the table and mediate their cases instead of litigating. It was organized by Don Reder, a nonlawyer, who became one of the key mediators in this highly successful program. He eventually started his own firm, Dispute Resolution Services. It had a roster of professional mediators, mostly retired judges, and Don. Marketing people handled the phones, and administrators scheduled cases. It was quite an operation. When I called, my obvious interest touched a nerve, and Don invited me to spend a couple of days observing. I sat in literally every office of his business and watched his people work. I asked questions and sat in on mediations. Now I had a business model. There was nothing in California like this, and the experience really helped me understand where the market could go. It was an exciting time, and I couldn't wait to get started.

I had a young family, a wife and two small daughters, and I knew I had to sustain them, but my own vision wasn't about the money: it was about doing something I was called to do and felt I could do well. If I made money, great. If not, well, I had a lifetime ticket that allowed me to return to the grind of trial work.

I like innovation, and I like to be involved in creating things. Like other successful people in this field, I don't mind taking a risk. At that time, however, becoming a mediator was more about saving my life than it was about starting a new career. In my law practice, I felt I was becoming a slave to the bureaucracy of corporate America. I was losing my character, and fast.

For example, to make sure my corporate clients felt comfortable, I had to keep my office decor bland and nonthreatening. Standard furniture, conventional prints framed and hung on the wall, no personal effects to hint at my personality, nothing too extravagant—

an uninspiring picture calculated not to offend the sensibilities of a corporate bureaucrat. My office did put the clients at ease, but it didn't feel like home to me. I grew increasingly dispirited, and wished that instead of dragging myself to the office I could wake up every day inspired and motivated to go to work and feel good about myself. Time felt precious; I didn't want to waste another minute.

Mediation was my ticket out. It let me find my own voice and not be the voice of an industry, a hired gun. As I mediated one case after another, I began to find that I could have fun with the process, trying different approaches and expressing aspects of myself I hadn't even known were there. I soon discovered that I thrived on building the intimate relationships that develop in mediations. People trusted me; they wanted to reveal their secrets and goals, and my job was to help them realize these goals. I also discovered that I didn't mind dealing with the ambiguity that arose when I put myself in the center of the tug-of-war between the conflicting parties. I'm also an idea juggler; I like having a lot of balls in the air. So that part of the process—going from one room to the next, understanding how each party was thinking, trying to help them reach multiple goals—suited me perfectly. To make a long story short, I found my groove in mediation, and the money seemed to follow naturally.

When I began, I had a goal. And I told myself that if I wasn't moving forward and creating progress, I could always stop and go back to the practice of law. But every year I did make progress, even baby steps, so I kept going.

Growing a New Profession

Fortunately, I wasn't alone. I was one of a small group of people who were trying to change the prevailing mind-set—that the courthouse was the only option available to resolve a case—and create a new field of practice in the civil justice system: mediation. I immersed myself in the idea of putting mediation on the map in California and got involved with the brand-new Southern California Mediation Association (SCMA), which had started at Pepperdine University School of Law. I joined with others in the legislative efforts to require the largest court in the country—the Los Angeles Superior Court—to mandate the use of mediation in all civil actions, and I found a receptive audience in the courts, in the trial lawyers' association, and in the insurance industry. The courts were already leaning toward mediation because of the obvious advantage of closing cases faster, saving administrative costs, and generally giving their customers—the public—more client satisfaction. At that time they were beginning to explore the process with retired judges, using mediation as a kind of settlement conference. It was a start, but to my mind this was just scratching the surface of what the process could be.

From a business standpoint, I realized that if I could get the courts to accept the idea of mediation as a valid process in its own right, I would be there to catch the fruit that fell from the trees. So I got involved in educating lawyers and judges about the process, spending a lot of time trying to convince the California courts to mandate mediation. They generally thought this idea was something of an oxymoron, because mediation is voluntary by nature. How do you *force* people to negotiate? We argued that two other states, Texas and Florida, were already successfully mandating mediation. Clearly we needed to educate lawyers about the process quickly if we were going to get the ball rolling in California.

We knew that if we got lawyers involved in mediation, the process would sell itself. So we pushed hard for two or three years, an informal but relentless effort by a group of highly motivated and committed individuals—the SCMA, Pepperdine, the Los Angeles County Bar Association, community leaders—getting together and asking, What can we do to institutionalize this process?

This effort opened some important professional doors. More and more lawyers got to know and trust me, and that began to pay off in cases coming my way. A big personal turning point came 1992, when a large insurance company decided that it wanted to settle hundreds of cases at once and wanted one mediation firm to handle the whole thing. A request for proposal was sent out to various mediation providers, and I was selected. That introduced me to a lot of lawyers—one for each case. I got on the phone and invited trial lawyers to attend a voluntary mediation, with me serving as the impartial mediator. They were reluctant at first, but in the end 70 to 80 percent of the cases agreed to mediate, *and they all settled*— not so much because of my skills as a mediator, but because the insurance company was motivated to settle. These lawyers, however, gave me more credit than I was perhaps due, and started referring more business to me.

Personal Success in a Burgeoning Field

In 1994, the field really took off when a group of ambitious mediators got the California court system to sign off on mandated mediation as a new law in Los Angeles County. The same year, I also became affiliated with Pepperdine University, where I had done a workshop in dispute resolution. After that, I was invited to teach a class and direct a six-day program called "Mediating the Litigated Case." Although I had never taught before, it seemed to come naturally and challenged me to stretch my abilities to connect with an audience, something all mediators need to do. Through that affiliation I was able to find institutional credibility in the marketplace: Pepperdine would regularly send out brochures about the course, with my picture prominently displayed, and it was terrific public relations at no cost to me. This was an unexpected bonus that helped me market myself and make money.

By 1996, I was fairly well known in the Southern California marketplace, and one of the few full-time mediators. In fact, the *Daily Journal*—read by every lawyer in Los Angeles—did a full-page profile about my practice called "A Full-Time Mediator Is a Rarity in California." In addition, I wrote a lot of articles for a variety of publications about mediation techniques and skills, learned to be a public speaker, became president of the SCMA—and all just because I truly enjoyed my work. It's great to wake up every day and look forward to what you're doing.

Today I'm making more money as a mediator than I did as a lawyer, yet ironically I'm more active in the law than I was when I was actually practicing law. I regularly read appellate decisions in order to stay updated on the various areas of the law I practice in, and I get to enjoy personal relationships with a wide variety of people. Like any entrepreneur, I have my ups and downs. If the phone doesn't ring for a day, I used to be concerned. Now I realize it's part of the rhythm of the business.

GETTING IN THE DOOR

Some mediators are seen as fringe players in the civil justice system until they become established. Other mediators, many with excellent skills, *never* become established. So the question is, what does it take to get established, to be the name that repeatedly shows up on the ledgers of people who are looking for mediators?

You need to begin by thinking of yourself as a professional mediator, believing in yourself, and living the part every day. You need to develop a reputation for mediating well and staying with a case until it closes. But beyond these fundamentals, you need to understand how to market yourself as a mediator: what it takes to get the power players on your side and what you need to do to be seen as—and become—part of their group.

To take a very simple example, I wear a suit and tie to work every day because when people go to court, they wear a suit and a conservative tie. I would be far more comfortable in khakis and an open-collar shirt, but I would also be viewed as a fringe player by the established players—lawyers—by whose good graces I survive. Because I want to be part of the established legal circle that views me as the head of the table, I dress accordingly. That doesn't mean I have to conduct the process in a staid and conservative manner— far from it. But dressing the part gets me in the door.

Here's another example. When I decide to write an article on mediation, I don't try to get it published on the op-ed page of the *Los Angeles Times*, but in the journals that my clients read every day.

I might reach thousands more with the *Times* article, but I won't be reaching the people who decide which mediator gets the case. Being perceived as an authority by potential clients gets me in the door.

The point is, do what you can to get in the door! Once you're inside the caucus room, you own it. You can work the room to your heart's content and be as creative and imaginative as you need to be to settle the case. But that involves another set of skills, not the ones we're talking about in this book.

Your ability to open the door and walk through it—your grasp on what it takes to market yourself as a mediator and manage your business well—will make or break your career. Making money as a mediator isn't the whole ball game, but it's a sign that your skills are recognized by your peers, that you have a high degree of business and marketing savvy, and that you're 100 percent committed to the practice of mediation. You've distinguished yourself from the mass of mediators and made it to the top: you've got the right stuff.

If you want to make money as a mediator—and achieve the success and satisfaction that come with the privilege of being able to work every day at a job you are passionate about—you'll do well to follow the models set by the thirty top mediators who were gracious enough to share the secrets of their success in this book. Nobody wants to give away the store to his or her competition, but the best mediators understand that they're not in competition with anyone but themselves. They understand that the practice of mediation is all about people and that sharing their wealth of knowledge and experience to help other talented people reach the top can only help the profession as a whole.

Every successful mediator I know—myself included—feels "lucky" to be able to work every day in a field as rewarding as this one. We all join in wishing you the very best of that luck in your chosen career.

1

Extreme Mediation
What Top-Tier Mediators Know That You Can Learn

> *I am as excited about my 3,700th mediation as I was about my first. This is a bring-your-A-game business. You have to be as strong on Friday as you are on Monday. If you make them know you are glad to see them and psyched for the task at hand, they'll be back.*
>
> Eric Galton

You're a natural: you know in your bones how to bring a room full of chaos and conflict to harmonious closure, and you just keep getting better and better. You've been a professional mediator for a while now, and there doesn't seem to be an upper limit to your improvement. You love what you do, and people want to be around you—you radiate energy. They'll even pay a lot of money to work with you and learn from you. You don't have to think about it: life is good. There's nothing else you would rather be doing.

This is how every single top-tier mediator I know experiences his or her profession. If this is how mediation makes you feel, you've got a real shot. But please note: these super-successful mediators are standing at the top of a pyramid that has a very broad base.

You've probably heard the 80-20 rule: 20 percent of the people do 80 percent of the work. That's as valid in mediation as it is anywhere, and perhaps more so. In mediation—whether it's commercial, employment, family law, dispute resolution, or any another

>
>
> ## You Gotta Have Heart
>
> You've got to have fun doing it. You have to have a passion. You put your energy where your heart is. You put your treasure where your heart is. If your interest is truly there, you put your resources there. Money will not give you a mediation business. It requires your time and effort in interacting with other people.
>
> *Robert Jenks*

specialty—the mediators on the bottom tier of the pyramid are constantly scrambling for work, losing heart, and returning to their former careers or searching for a new path. Those who do manage to rise up to the small middle tier—about 15 percent—stay busy, make a good living, but never quite break through. Meanwhile, the top 5 percent—for our purposes, the highest earners in a given region—have calendars that are filled months in advance and bank accounts that are bulging at the seams.

Some of this success depends on one's niche. It's no surprise that mediators who work primarily on panels or part-time or in family law or neighborhood disputes are unlikely ever to see the kind of money that a full-time mediator who settles multiparty construction cases brings in regularly—even if their negotiation skills and personalities are in every other way equal. That may not seem fair, but—at least for now—that's the way the mediation market is set up.

Mediation is an extreme career. Many describe it as a calling. It's a field in which you *can* be wildly successful—think Tiger Woods, Martina Navritolova, Lance Armstrong—but only a relative few make it to that top tier and thrive. Those who do can't imagine doing anything else. Like Paul Monicatti of Michigan, they say, "Mediation is my passion, and it is also so much fun for me that if I didn't have to pay bills, I'd do it for free."

If you can say the same, then you've found your calling as a mediator. If you don't have the energy, the love, the passion for mediation that the top people have, the truth is that you'll probably never join them.

FALLING OFF THE MEDIATOR BANDWAGON

It seems as though everybody wants to jump on the mediator bandwagon these days. As New Orleans mediator Robert Jenks says wryly, "You can't swing a cat without hitting a mediator, but you can swing a lot of cats without hitting a good mediator." Toronto's Cliff Hendler agrees: "Virtually every lawyer who appears before me in mediation says, 'I could do that.'" And in Minnesota, Michael Landrum says, "I can't remember the last time I was in a mediation when one of the lawyers didn't say, 'Well, I'm a mediator too!'" I, too, have had this experience many times over.

Not surprisingly, our profession is packed with people who are trying to get a piece of the ever-expanding mediation pie. If you're a mediator, you've probably been through at least some basic mediation training. The number of trainers and programs seems to be exploding, and they are turning out hopeful new mediators almost daily. For many would-be mediators, this career choice seems like a no-brainer. Unlike the person getting a credential to become a teacher or a law degree to become a lawyer, or putting in years of study to become a doctor, you don't need years of dedicated schooling and a special degree to set up a practice. And look at the payoff: the most successful mediators are shining examples of what might be—they're making a lot of money, they seem to enjoy their work, and they make it look easy.

Only a Few Survive

The mediation pie can expand, but the number of people eating that pie expands geometrically. So if business doubles, we've got quadruple the number of people wanting to be mediators. But only a small number of people are going to sustain themselves as mediators long term in the private sector. The volume of people interested in being mediators is always going to exceed the number who are really able to do it.

I think too many people go out there and train as a source of income—and you can make an okay amount of money. If people are taking the training to skill enhance, that's fine. But I get a résumé once a week from a person who says, "I've just been through mediation training; I want to get into this field. Do you have any jobs for me? If you don't, can you give me advice?" And I do give them advice. But the truth is, making a good living in mediation is a very difficult thing to do.

Robert A. Creo

Crash! Most of the freshly minted newcomers who burst out of basic programs raring to go stumble at the first gate. What they're stumbling over is their own skewed idea of the reality of a mediator's life and what it takes to achieve success.

The first hard lesson newcomers learn is that experience and success count for a lot in this business, and they have yet to acquire it. Southern California mediator Nina Meierding says, "I receive dozens of calls from people who want to 'take me out to lunch' so that I can tell them how to be an instant success. The brutal reality is that there is no instant success—it takes commitment, a

Field of Dreams

I, too, initially had the *Field of Dreams* approach: "If I build it (mediation), they (the public) will come." I believed that the concept of mediation was so good and so right that anyone would immediately see its value. This is not true. The need for mediation is greater than the demand; and if you are to make your career in mediation, you must be strategic, thoughtful, thorough, and self-evaluative in your approach.

Nina Meierding

healthy dose of risk tolerance, a solid business perspective, and faith in yourself." Chris Moore, who specializes in dispute resolution at CDR Associates in Boulder, Colorado, says, "One of the things that makes the biggest difference is a track record. Which means that it's harder for a new mediator to leap in and have a successful business. You need to estimate that it's going to be about five years before you have a sustainable practice—if you get there."

Five years?

For Geoff Sharp, a successful commercial mediator in Wellington, New Zealand, the first few years were anything but glamorous. "My story," he says, "involves lonely days at the afternoon movies in my first year of practice, wearing suits to an empty office and putting the kids' school fees on Visa. Seven years later it involves doing rewarding work in my chosen field and telling wannabe mediators to get staunch, do the hard yards, and realize this is no ordinary profession with established pathways to practice."

Getting a track record of successful settlements entails having clients—and that means courting contacts, and that means getting out there and doing the hard marketing: selling yourself, but in the most effective and personable way possible. And, for many, it also means learning how to run a business and keep it going on a very short shoestring. Often it means working more hours than you sleep and staying sharp enough to do it all again the next day.

The majority of people who say, "Hey, I could do that!" and complete a forty-hour basic mediation course quickly discover that making a living in this profession is not nearly as easy as it looks from the outside. In fact, it's not easy at all. Sooner or later, those for whom the hard work outweighs the fun drop away.

NOT FOR THE FAINT OF HEART

As the old saying goes, "Many are called; few are chosen." Pursuing a truly successful mediation career is not for the faint of heart. As Geoff Sharp says, mediation is no ordinary profession—and there is no one golden road to success, financial or otherwise. Each of the relative handful of super-successful mediators has his or her own road story to tell. Some left successful litigation practices because helping people resolve disputes without rancor felt better than arguing one side over the other. Philadelphia lawyer-turned-mediator Ben Picker recalls, "I became a lawyer primarily because of my desire to work with individuals in a collaborative effort to solve their problems. Until I began my mediation practice, the greatest satisfaction I received from the practice of law was from my work on public interest and pro bono matters. As a mediator, far more so than when I was a trial lawyer, I engage in a collaborative effort to solve problems and in a process where the people are as important as the issues. As a consequence, I feel more than at any other time in my professional life that I am adding value to the profession."

Some, like former insurance professional Cliff Hendler, left actuarial or accounting careers because they found a truer calling in working with people around the same issues they used to resolve on paper. Others, like Chris Moore's business partner Bernie Mayer, found their way to mediation and dispute resolution from the helping professions—teaching, social work, psychotherapy—bringing their training and sensibilities to resolving personal or community disputes or to working with social issues on a larger scale.

All, however, have what has been called a "unique ability" for mediation. They are passionate about what they do, and doing it comes naturally. If you agree with all—not merely most—of the following statements, you're echoing the feelings of every top-tier mediator I know:

- I love mediating, and I'm energized by it.

- It's easy. When I'm in the middle of a mediation, everything flows.

- I always get good results, and I often get better results than I'm expecting.

- I experience personal growth from my work in mediation. The more time I spend on it, the more powerful it becomes.

- I get positive feedback from clients and colleagues about my work.

- Mediating, thinking about mediating, and being a mediator give me an overall feeling of satisfaction.

- I can't imagine being happy doing anything else for a living.

Successful mediators enjoy meeting new people, talking with them, and learning about them. They get energy from social interaction and seek it out. Most intuitively understand "how to make friends and influence people." In some sense they are salespeople,

Doing Good and Doing Well

The major reason that I and my colleagues at CDR Associates entered this field was our values about resolving disputes, not to get rich. We wanted to promote effective collaborative decision making and support the peaceful resolution of serious differences.

For me, I can do work that is related to social justice and building peace and it's congruent with my values—and I can make a living at it. It's pretty amazing. But I am not alone in this. Most of the people in this field are very value driven.

The people I know who work in the public policy and dispute resolution field have a very high level of value motivation. They're concerned about the issues in the arena they work in. They're also concerned about developing collaborative solutions, solutions that are transparent and cost-effective, and they see it also as a way of promoting democracy—it's a nonadversarial form of democratic decision making that meshes with more traditional legislative or administrative decision making. The level of participation by key parties, the quality of input, and the degree that customized integrative solutions are developed that have consensus support make outcomes far superior to normal legislative or administrative decision-making processes.

Chris Moore

and the product they are selling is peace between parties. Surprisingly—or perhaps not so surprisingly—many describe themselves as "conflict averse." They may be hotshot negotiators, juggling five parties with five points of view and getting them to settle, but they'd rather pay sticker price for a new car and drive it off the lot than haggle with the dealer to get the best deal. Often that's the reason for leaving a law practice. They receive much more satisfaction from helping parties reach a mutually satisfying resolution than from ensuring that one party "wins" a case at the expense of another.

WHAT TOP-TIER MEDIATORS HAVE IN COMMON

If you aspire to a flourishing, lucrative practice in the field of mediation or dispute resolution, you will do well to emulate the men and women who are in that position right now. In my experience, top-tier mediators have the following in common:

- We love to mediate, and we're very good at our job.

- We inspire trust.

- We cultivate champions, developing relationships with people who are in a position to refer cases.

- We work hard.

- We charge more than the going rate, even for routine cases.

We'll look more closely at all of these—and other important issues, including marketing, business models, money, and more—throughout this book. Right now, let's touch on each of these

An Undiluted Passion

Dwelling in the field of mediation, as I have since 1988, has been not only a source of intense interest but an undiluted passion for me. What is it about this new but really very old form of conflict resolution that seems to still have me firmly in its grip? While it is true that I am paid well, particularly when mediating large complex and multiparty cases, it's certainly not just the money.

Prestige? While I have had my hotshot periods, mediating flashy cases and fending off the press, being president of this and that, I seem to be learning some humility. While I used to say, "I settled that case," I now understand that I'm really a guest, managing the process with as light a hand as possible, and it's the parties and their lawyers who settle cases in mediation, not me.

"I dwell in possibility—/ A fairer house than prose—/ More numerous of windows / Superior—for Doors—." These lines from Emily Dickinson got me thinking about what it is that fascinates me so much about mediation. Much of the allure, the kick, the deep satisfaction and insight into the human psyche as we struggle with conflict is . . . the abundant presence of possibility, all those windows and doors offering creative paths not just to resolution, but sweet closure, sometimes life-altering relief; the tantalizing choice in the settle-litigate decision between certainty or uncertainty. Getting to be a part of all this, each case and the cast of characters different from the last, getting to experience the human drama of change: a "fairer house" indeed.

Harry Goodheart

fundamental factors and what top-tier mediators have to say about their work.

We Love to Mediate

Harry Goodheart, working in Florida and North Carolina, has been a successful mediator for more than seventeen years. Even after nearly three thousand mediations, in addition to trainings and seminars, he calls his practice "an undiluted passion." Like most successful mediators, it's not just the money that brought him to mediation and keeps him there.

Money is the scorecard, but it can't be the whole ball game. Along with most mediators I know, I have worked pro bono if a dispute calls for it. A few years ago, for example, I was struck by a photo of a family on the cover of a legal publication. The parents claimed that their son had been discriminated against on his high school baseball team because he was Jewish. This dispute between the family and the school and the coach had entered high-powered litigation; the lawyers representing the family were from one of the top firms in Los Angeles, and they were handling the case pro bono. The case appealed to me—I was Jewish, I was a mediator, I had attended Dodger fantasy camp—and I felt that I might be able to help. I decided to call the lawyers both for the family and for the coach and the school district to see if there was anything I could do. The lawyers knew of me, and they were happy to accept my offer to mediate the case pro bono. We were able to avoid court, settle the case, and smooth out some emotional issues for all the parties. It was a very satisfying experience for me and the kind of case that I strongly feel those of us who are in the top tier should be taking on more often.

Ultimately, the only true measure of success is our own sense of satisfaction. But unless we are truly and purely altruistic, that personal feeling of success will be reflected in a more tangible outer success: we will make a good or even great living doing what we love to do.

I View My Work as a Calling

I am not entirely sure why I have been successful while other very talented mediators have struggled, but I would guess that these are the contributing factors:

1. I genuinely like working with lawyers, have been very active in the bar, and am relatively well known among lawyers. I was president of the county bar association and have served on the board of bar examiners and on lots of bar committees. I have done plenty of Continuing Legal Education (CLE) speaking, and I continue to do so.

2. I regularly advertise in bar publications and occasionally write articles. My ads are simple reminders that I am available and are not full of the usual adjectives. They include a photo. I find that when I meet people for the first time, they recognize me and seem to know me because of the ad.

3. I treat nearly every contact I have with lawyers and businesspeople in the community as a potential opportunity to explain what I do and how I can be of service.

4. I view my work as a calling and am dedicated to lifelong learning and improvement. I try to treat each case, no matter how mundane, as an opportunity to provide a service that uniquely suits the needs of the parties. The feedback I receive from lawyers seems to indicate that they notice and appreciate this.

Susan Hammer

We Inspire Trust

Perhaps the most important key to being a successful mediator is that your clients and potential clients—whether they are lawyers, helping professionals, families, or community leaders—feel they can trust you to be fair and to help them grapple with the life-changing issues that arise in mediated negotiations.

All top-tier mediators will tell you that inspiring trust is paramount. "The mediator must be able to find connections with the parties so that they feel like this person can help them work through

---

The Biggest Fear

The biggest fear most people have is that they'll be taken advantage of. So any marketing message must include the emotional appeal, "You will not be played for a fool in my office."

Most of what mediators are taught is self-defeating. In many situations one or the other of the parties feel they'll be at a decided disadvantage. If you talk to a mediator and you feel you're not a good negotiator, and the mediator says, "I'm going to be *neutral*," you'll feel that you're going to get screwed. Mediators have been taught to say this, and it sounds good, but it scares the hell out of people.

Good mediators can overcome that because they have a presence, despite their words, that people can trust. The best mediators know how to pick up on cues that a person is anxious, and they work to sell the message, "You're not going to lose in this mediation."

Robert Benjamin

difficult issues—a personal bond," explains Chris Moore. "If people are going to be in a lifeboat on a stormy sea, they want someone with them they trust and have some connection with. But they also don't expect you to be totally partial to them—they expect you to be fair. And they hope you can help them talk to the other side, people whom they have historically found to be difficult to talk with. You facilitate and design a process that helps them talk *and* reach agreements."

In my own work, I try to cultivate trust in all my interactions with potential clients, from first contact to final settlement. At the outset, when they inquire if I can help, I begin by talking to them, asking questions almost as a doctor would, trying to "diagnose" their conflict by learning more about what's driving it. And I listen. Often mediators assume they need to "sell" themselves to clients. But when you let others do the talking, you're showing concern for their pain and respecting their needs—you're not trying to sell them anything. By the end of the conversation they understand that you care and that you can solve their problem. And once you've gained their trust and they've booked a place on your calendar, you do everything you can to ensure that you keep their trust throughout the mediation process.

We Cultivate Champions

A passion for mediating and terrific natural skills can take you only so far. You need to cultivate champions—influential people who believe in you as a mediator and who are more than happy to help you get your name out there to larger groups. I have been fortunate enough to have had several important champions who paved the way for me, introducing me to important potential clients and polishing my reputation. If you have even one such champion, you can consider yourself fortunate indeed. But note: they will not always come into your life by chance. You need to cultivate these relationships.

Early in my career, I met and made friends with a lawyer who was known as the "godfather" of employment law, a really powerful

Success

There are different kinds of success. For some people, having a job that allows you to focus on your chosen work is successful. Making a lot of money is another kind of success (although, as a social worker and the child of two social workers, I've never had that as a goal). For me, what's successful is that I am able in my work to help people deal with the conflicts they're facing. Successful means that people ask me to provide help that is constructive and appropriate to their situation, and that I am able to provide that help and make a living by doing so.

Bernie Mayer

force in this area. He saw right away that mediation was a good thing, and I thought he might be a champion for me in the employment arena. He had an organization of like-minded employment lawyers, and from time to time he invited me to their meetings to speak about mediation. I couldn't have asked for a better platform or intermediary. He was an influential person among a lot of people. Having this respected professional singing my praises and introducing me to potential clients was much more effective than any number of cold calls I might have made.

I am lucky to have another of my champions on *my* side; being on the bad side of powerful and influential people can be an instant career killer. Once a year, a couple of lawyers I am friendly with invite about five hundred trial lawyers to a big meeting where they do a blow-by-blow review of all the arbitrators and mediators in town—and by now there are hundreds of them. Still, they go through them one by one, saying, "Stay away from this one" or "This one's great." Fortunately, they have always recommended me at these meetings, and that has gone a long way toward encouraging others to try my services. After a while, more and more people retained me as their mediator, until I reached a critical mass in the marketplace and became established. Being established is the breakthrough everyone in this business strives to achieve.

We Work Hard

Many newcomers to mediation think it's going to be an easy way to make a buck—or at least a lot easier than the career they want to leave. But successful mediators, virtually without exception, work hard—all day and almost every day. Rod Max practices in Alabama and Florida. He says, "There are a lot of individuals who want to be mediators. They're great lawyers, judges, businesspeople—but to establish the network that gets you cases and fills your calendar takes a lot of work. A lot of work! I have dedicated myself to working this on an everyday basis. I'm motivated to assist lawyers and their clients."

"You have to be committed," says Toronto's Rick Weiler. "Lots of people are getting certified, but the vast majority fall by the wayside because they think it looks easy—access to the field is easy, and mediators look like they have it made. But they're not prepared to do what's necessary to get to the point where they would be broadly acceptable to a critical mass of lawyers. It's about understanding how the process works and being prepared to commit to it. It's like anything else. If you are setting the goal for yourself that you will be in the top 5 percent, you have to work hard, develop a strategy, continually upgrade your skills, and have the drive to keep going."

"You can't do this part-time and be successful," explains Pittsburgh mediator Robert A. Creo. "The people who are really successful work hard."

On the Power of Persistence

Successful mediators are persistent—they hang in there, doing what it takes for as long as it takes to make sure every mediation settles. This tenacity carries over to their career as a whole. Despite setbacks, during lean years, they persevere, doing what they need to do to ensure they stay in the field and enjoy growing success.

One of the biggest criticisms I hear is that a mediator gives up too soon. Good ones follow up with phone calls, a second session—they hang in there. They have tenacity.

Michael Landrum

I work hard and know what I'm doing. People know that I will work really hard to get a case settled. Their past experience with me and my reputation tell them that I'm committed to the people and the process.

Cliff Hendler

Perseverance and following up are critical factors for mediators. People hire me because I won't give up on a case. Even if a case doesn't settle on the day, people know I'll stick with it and follow up.

Rick Weiler

A Day in the Life

One of the ongoing challenges of a full-time mediator is the calendar. During travel and breaks, I return telephone calls, follow up on unsettled cases, and communicate with my office via cell phone. My phone has a voicemail. I have my office call me to leave substantive messages when I am out. I respond via telephone or email when the schedule permits it. Here's my calendar for one recent Monday:

9 A.M.–noon: Mediation of a two-party personal injury claim involving a woman injured in an auto accident.

12:15–1:30 P.M.: Meeting of the bar association dispute resolution committee.

2:00–4:00 P.M.: Adjunct professor teaching international dispute resolution at the University of Pittsburgh School of Law.

4:30–6:00 P.M.: Meeting with the University of Pittsburgh Medical Center risk management team to review upcoming educational conferences for lawyers and submission of new cases to mediation.

6:00–7:00 P.M.: Quick meal and travel. Return calls on the road.

7:00–8:00 P.M.: Presentation on asymmetry in mediation to Western Pennsylvania Council of Mediators.

8:30–10:00 P.M.:	Watch TV show *24*; read *New York Times*.
10:00–11:00 P.M.:	Review submissions for next day's case.
11:30 P.M.–midnight:	Review and respond to emails.

Robert A. Creo

We Charge More Money

It's no secret: the most successful mediators charge more money than the middle tier of mediators in their region. When parties are truly committed to settling a large case, they are willing to pay what it takes to get the job done. And when people like to say that you're a mediator who always gets the job done, you have every reason to be paid what you are worth. That's why the top 5 percent of mediators charge in the top range of fees, and that's why they get it.

Counterintuitive? Yes. But if you can back up your fee schedule with results, it works. Clients are often more than willing to commit to a higher-priced mediator with a great reputation because they want to make sure the job gets done right. For the very same reason, you're more likely to hire a higher-priced but guaranteed excellent firm of builders to remodel your kitchen. And you're certainly going to look for the best orthopedist in town to repair your knee—hang the cost. Admittedly, there's some degree of snob appeal involved. Just as many lawyers prefer to be seen driving BMWs rather than Toyotas, they also prefer to tell their clients that they've signed up "the best mediator in the business"—and point to your fee schedule to back up their claim.

Setting high fees takes a bit of fearlessness—you must be willing to lose some business in order to get a different kind of case.

Do You Have What It Takes to Be a Success?

1. **Successful mediators love to mediate, and they are very good at their job.**

   You live, breathe, eat, and sleep mediation. You'd rather be mediating than doing any other job. Mediating gives you intense satisfaction, and you get better at it every day. If this describes you, super success may be within your reach.

2. **Successful mediators are likeable and inspire trust.**

   You enjoy people, and people enjoy being around you. Clients, former clients, and prospective clients give you continual feedback about how great you are at your job, how many good things they've heard about your work, how safe they feel about putting their clients' lives in your hands. If you can inspire this level of trust, you might make it to the top tier.

3. **Successful mediators cultivate champions: they make relationships with people who are in a position to refer cases.**

   You understand intuitively who will be able to help you expand your network, and you actively seek out relationships with them. You create a mutual admiration society that spills over into all of your champion's social contacts. If people are hearing good things about you from influential others, your business should increase exponentially.

4. Successful mediators work hard.

You work hard in mediations to ensure a successful outcome for everyone, and you work hard outside mediations to build your network of contacts, market your business, increase your knowledge and skill base, and share your expertise with others. You understand that a career in mediation is not for those who enjoy long vacations and twelve hours of sleep every night, and you wake every morning eager to get to work.

5. Successful mediators charge more than the going rate, even for routine cases.

You know your fees are higher than what other mediators around you are charging, but you're worth it. If clients want you—that is, if they want their case settled by the best mediator in business—they'll understand that paying your fee is an investment in a successful settlement.

Rick Weiler says, "I price myself aggressively for our market, so I don't get the garden-variety case. The people hiring me believe there's a special reason to pay more for me." And Cliff Hendler says, "I charge a lot of money. I priced myself out of the smaller-end market. I concentrate on bigger cases. And it works—people pay it."

GETTING TO THE TOP

No matter how high he or she rises, every mediator starts in the same place: at the bottom. Simply getting started in the business is basic math: you begin with one case and meet two lawyers. If you're successful, those two lawyers tell more lawyers about you. Your business

How to Have a Successful Career as a Mediator

Be open to opportunities. Be willing to invest your time and capital. Be patient. Give back. The best thing you can do, in spite of all the above, is to do good work as a mediator. If it's meant to be, it will be.

Tracy Allen

picks up, you schedule and settle more and more cases, and somewhere along the line—breakthrough! You've reached a critical mass in your contacts, and the ripe fruit is dropping off the trees and into your hands.

Is it that simple? No, far from it. If you want to climb to the very top of the pyramid, you're going to have to put some of your life on hold and pour massive amounts of energy into achieving that goal. It's not easy, and it doesn't happen overnight. If this sounds like some kind of fun, welcome to the club!

TOP-TIER STRATEGIES

1. **Be willing to work hard.**

    If you want to be among the most successful mediators, you must be willing to narrow your focus and devote a tremendous amount of energy toward your goal. This means early mornings, late nights, busy days, and—at least in the beginning—less time to spend with family and friends.

2. Never give up.

The road to success is not straight and sure, and it doesn't happen overnight. If you begin your career by accepting the fact that will be working toward your goal for a few hard years, you will be much more likely to persevere and—eventually!—reach the top.

3. If mediation is not your passion, find another career.

If you are not willing to eat, sleep, and dream mediation—and enjoy virtually every minute of it—you will not be able to stay the course long enough to become a highly successful mediator. Think about this seriously: If you have the passion and dedication real success in the business takes, welcome to the club!

2

Be Yourself

Inspiring Trust, Projecting Authenticity, Honing Your Skills

Who you are as an individual and your approach toward conflict are hugely important. People want to spend a day with someone they want to spend a day with.

Cliff Hendler

A few years ago, I found myself overbooked, and I recommended a fellow mediator, Bill, to take over a case I couldn't fit on my schedule. I'd never seen him in action, but I knew he settled cases, and I felt confident that he could handle this one. After the case settled, I ran into one of the lawyers on the case.

"How did Bill work out for you?" I asked.

The lawyer looked uncomfortable. "Well," he replied, "the case settled. But I don't think we'll be using Bill again."

"Really? Why not?" I knew this was a complex case, and I'd heard that he'd handled it well.

"Frankly," the lawyer said, "I just couldn't stand the guy. He knows what he's doing, and the parties seemed satisfied, but he just didn't come across as all that genuine to me. Sorry."

You can have A-1 mediation skills, you may understand other people, you may have booked speaking engagements far into the future, and you may even settle a fair number of cases that come your way—and you can still find yourself with an empty calendar because people just can't seem to relate to you as a person. Being a successful and highly paid mediator is not just about what you do in the mediation room. It's a whole package—doing the work, getting the clients, keeping the clients, getting more clients, and keeping the whole ball rolling—and what holds this package together and gives it life is *you*. If you—the genuine human being inside the mediator suit—are not truly present in every encounter, inside or outside the conference room, you will find it difficult if not impossible to succeed in this highly competitive profession. One mediator puts it simply: "The best advice I can give you is, 'Be yourself.'"

YOU ARE WHAT YOU'VE GOT TO OFFER

Mediation is an unusually personal profession. Good cardiac specialists with an abrasive beside manner still manage to find patients, and CPAs who can do complicated tax work but have trouble carrying on a conversation find plenty of business. But mediators who have a broad grasp of theoretical knowledge and have learned advanced mediation skills, yet don't click with people, will never find much success. "Mediation is a people-oriented and personality-driven business," says Los Angeles mediator Steve Cerveris. "Attorneys often come to us because they respect us and because we can effectively relate to and communicate with their clients and with them."

As every mediator soon learns, there's nothing cut and dried about our field. You're dealing with grief, hurt feelings, great loss—almost no matter what the subject of dispute is, deep emotions are involved, and they all have to be resolved before the case settles, whether it's a divorce, a malpractice suit, or a highly complex water rights issue.

As a mediator you must make a personal connection with everyone in the room. At the end of every successful settlement, you've shared a piece of yourself. "You're meshing your energy with other

Build Trust

It takes many good experiences to build trust, but only one to blow it. Do your homework.

Gary Furlong

---

people's energy, and possibly changing their life," says Alabama mediator Michelle Obradovic.

Clients book you for a case because they want to hire you specifically. They feel that *you* are the one mediator who can see them through their dispute. This means that you can't just be an image of what you think you should be. You've got to be comfortable in your own skin and be able to project that comfort outward. How do you do that? Square one: be true to yourself. Be yourself. Apply the experience that comes with doing cases day in and day out. People will sense your sincerity and continue to use you.

TRUST, TRUST, TRUST

As everyone knows, the key factor in real estate is location, location, location. In mediation, it's trust, trust, trust. "The main quality parties look for in a mediator," says Oregon mediator Susan Hammer, "is someone they trust and think is fair, someone they feel regards them in a positive light." The following sample of how satisfied clients describe their experience with successful mediators, taken from the Web sites of some of this book's contributors, reflects this feeling. People respond to these mediators on a personal level and trust them to handle what may be the most critical hours in their lives with respect and care:

> "[She was] fair and balanced in her approach to both of us. She made the divorce process manageable in the midst of our chaos and sadness."
>
> "Thank you for your efforts yesterday. I appreciate your candor, sensitivity and wisdom. I think your gentle guidance throughout the day made all the difference in the world, both in terms of a fair resolution and allowing my clients to get through a very difficult process."
>
> "[His] patience and insight are invaluable."
>
> "[He] takes cases personally and he does his very best to try to get them resolved amicably."
>
> "It was truly a pleasure meeting you. You have an excellent rapport with people."

The importance of trust in our business cannot be overstated. Mediators work to ensure that the parties, who invariably begin the negotiation suspicious of one another and fearful of being taken advantage of, move steadily toward a position of mutual trust that brings settlement. If the parties do not feel they can trust you, they will stubbornly hold to their positions. And if, upon meeting you, they intuitively feel they can't trust you, they will not hire you. Period.

A mediator who inspires trust is halfway to settling before the negotiation even begins. "A good mediator can overcome people's innate fear of being taken for a fool because they have a presence that people can trust," explains Robert Benjamin. "The best mediators know how to pick up on cues that a person is anxious, and know that they need to sell the idea that 'You're not going to lose or compromise any interest you may have in this mediation.'

From Lawyer to Mediator

After twenty-five years of trial practice, two factors came together to cause me to look in other career directions. The first was a comment from a client whom I ran into a year after getting the best trial and appellate result I had ever obtained for a client: "I don't really even want to talk to you, John," he said. "Seeing you reminds me of the worst time of my life."

"Don, I don't understand. We got everything we asked for."

"No, John, *you* got everything you asked for. But I don't remember you ever asking me what I wanted."

The second factor grew out of a litigation team meeting where our insurance defense team reported that our clients were paying outside firms to audit our bills. That, of course, would only occur if our clients did not fully trust us.

In the late 1980s, concerned about the remedy-specific nature of litigation and the growing client concerns, I started researching alternatives and, of course, came across the growing literature about mediation. I then began efforts, along with many others, that culminated in our state supreme court's adopting rules that allowed trial judges to order parties to mediation.

John Van Winkle

"Parties in a mediation are very much like horses," he explains. "They are prey animals, ready to run at the first perceived false move or threat. If you understand this, you can approach your parties the way a horse whisperer might approach an untamed horse, slowly and firmly—using their nature, not fighting it. If you have to have the parties' buy-in, then you have to find a way to 'tame' them without breaking their spirit, to get them to relax enough that they can consider shifting their perspective."

What will backfire every time is simply pretending to be nice. Earning trust is not about agreeing with everything your client tells you. It involves being open to learning their objectives, and confirming to them that you understand their viewpoint. From there you can give them an authentic assessment and provide direction and leadership.

AUTHENTICITY

Authenticity is the bedrock on which trust is built, but it can be a tricky concept to explain. People perceive you as being authentic as a mediator when everything about you says that you are working from your deepest values and will do everything in your power to ensure that everyone in the room is treated fairly. At first hearing, this seems fairly straightforward. But, as Robert Benjamin explains, "This stuff is a hell of a lot more ambiguous and in a shifting conflict terrain than most people want to admit."

Every top-tier mediator understands the necessity of ensuring that people trust you without question even as you engage in the unavoidable manipulation and deception that are inherently part of every successful settlement process. The best mediators will tell you that, ultimately, they are prepared to do whatever works to help the parties settle.

Does this mean we're dishonest? I don't think so. We're all guilty of some form of deception every day. Turning down a dinner invitation with a false excuse; answering "Fine" when a coworker asks, "How are you doing?" when in fact you are having a tough day; or offering thanks for a gift that you really don't want are all considered acceptable forms of deception. Our culture reinforces the idea that telling a white lie is preferable to blunt truth if it results in a positive outcome. Deception is tolerated in negotiations because there, too, it can be used constructively and productively to develop concessions that lead to agreement.

Benjamin has thought and written extensively about authenticity. He points out, "Although authenticity requires some measure of honesty, it is not necessarily congruent with being scrupulously honest all of the time. Although authenticity is essential to build trust, it may well be that people recognize that they may need to be deceived and expect and tolerate some measure of artful sleight-of-hand to help them manage."

Here's an example that should be familiar to most mediators. The plaintiff's attorney in an insurance case tells me that they're ready to settle right now for $1 million. But the insurer has already told me in confidence that he's authorized to offer up to a cap of $2 million. Now, I could just carry the $1 million offer to the insurer, and both parties would be happy—for the moment, at least. Ethically, I can't tell the plaintiff that the insurer is ready to go $2 million and to hold out for more. My main concerns are that everyone is treated fairly, that the deal is settled amicably, and that no one feels cheated. So far, I've worked hard to build a reservoir of trust, and I'm pretty sure I can keep both parties with me until we reach a more equitable settlement. I choose to keep the mediation rolling. My strategy is to conduct a full-blown hearing, which gives everyone the sense that he or she has been heard. A hearing is not actually necessary for me in terms of understanding the case, but if I were to short-circuit the process and split the baby, somebody might feel that he or she has left something on the table. When I then break up into private caucus sessions, I am very comfortable directing the negotiation and making suggestions about what people should ask for and offer so that the settlement ultimately occurs in a range that is equally satisfying to both sides.

Is it strictly honest? No. Is it authentic? Absolutely. We all leave with a good feeling. Plaintiff and defendant feel fairly treated and confident that no money was left on the table. And I enjoyed keeping all

The Operating Definition of Authenticity

Many people confuse authenticity with "honesty" or living out of your "authentic self." But this denies the fact that, in life as well as in mediation, self-delusion and deception are inescapable. In mediation, the operating definition of authenticity is your ability to connect with people, gain their trust, and build up that kind of capital so that when you ask them to consider doing something they are resistant to, they will do it.

Robert Benjamin

the balls in the air as long as necessary and catching them all safely as they dropped.

Benjamin illustrates perhaps the ultimate example of projecting authenticity with the story of Terry Waite, a hostage negotiator who was later taken hostage himself. In 1983, Waite was asked to negotiate the release of a British hostage with Libyan leader Colonel Moammar Gadhafi, generally considered to be an "evildoer" and "madman." In fact, his first meeting with the Libyan leader compelled Waite to cross a stadium filled with the bodies of people Gadhafi had had killed. Waite, a devoutly religious man, could not find moral ground with Gadhafi. But he was able to put his personal beliefs aside and find his authenticity in a deep commitment to principle: he did not want play anyone for a fool, even Gadhafi. And the colonel could see that this was true. And because Waite sincerely wanted the hostages released, he was able to strategically empathize with Gadhafi.

This is a subtle point—we're not talking Machiavelli here; the ends don't always justify the means. Your authenticity is not rooted in your commitment to absolute truth or to always telling each party exactly what the other is thinking. Rather, it's rooted in your sincere desire to get the best settlement possible for all parties and in your commitment to seeing the process through to the end. The very best mediators feel this, mean it, and project it in everything they do. As Steve Cerveris says, "A lot of PR and spin goes on, but if it's not from the gut, parties will sense it."

FOLLOW YOUR OWN PATH

One reason mediation is so much fun is that it encourages creativity and innovation. The "man in the gray flannel suit" mentality is not a part of our image. The best mediators, in fact, are known for their unique qualities, reflected in their sometimes twisting career paths. "I worked for five years as an actor with an emphasis on comedy," says Toronto's Gary Furlong, "then produced theatre for two years, then moved to the States and worked as a mortgage broker for five years, started consulting in customer service and organizational effectiveness, and then became a mediator and got a Master of Laws. You know—the normal career path."

Well-known mediator Tony Piazza has a background in law and a third-degree black belt in Aikido, "a Japanese martial art based on principles of resolving conflict without escalating violence." Nina Meierding uses her background as both a trial lawyer and a schoolteacher to get to the heart of family mediations. London's Tony Willis, probably one of the most respected mediators worldwide, was previously the head of one the major litigation firms in the United Kingdom. Other top mediators have their own stories of finding their place in mediation.

"I started practicing law in 1976 in general commercial litigation in a large law firm," says Susan Hammer. "After doing litigation for a few years, I thought, 'There has to be a better way to solve problems. It's so lucrative for the lawyers and generally so unsatisfying for the clients.' I also saw a lot of cases where the conflict

>
>
> ## You Have to Know Something About Something
>
> You have to have a substantive background. Insurance, medicine, law—and just because you're a lawyer doesn't mean you have a strong background. You have to *know* something about something. People look to have a problem solved by someone who is an expert in a certain area. You have to know the area. And, of course, you also have to have contacts in that area.
>
> *Cliff Hendler*

between the lawyers was kind of a hobby for the lawyers that the clients were paying for. It seemed to me like a bad deal.

"So," she continues, "I started doing unconventional things like making an appointment with opposing counsel and trying to settle up front—breaking though conventional barriers. It was remarkably successful! At that time people were paying lip service to mediation, but the field had not yet begun in earnest, so I didn't really think I could do this as a career. I trained as a mediator in 1988 and mediated maybe one case a month. For the next ten years I went to seminars on mediation, but I continued to litigate. Finally, in 1998, I left the law firm and started my own mediation practice."

Draw from Your Strength

Many—some say far too many!—came to mediation from careers in litigation or as retired judges. Even though I have to admit to a personal bias toward law and the belief that a good mediator needs to understand the law, I am the first to admit that not every great mediator is also a lawyer. Cliff Hendler capitalized on his background in insurance claims handling to mediate insurance litigation, and parlayed that experience into mediating complex cases ranging from medical malpractice to sexual harassment. Chris Moore has a Ph.D. in political sociology and development, focused his graduate work on dispute resolution techniques, and enjoys an amazing career settling environmental, organizational, and international disputes. Bernie Mayer began as a social worker and psychotherapist. All of them scaled the pyramid by drawing on their own field of knowledge and pool of contacts to create a unique niche and a satisfying career.

"I became successful because I came in early on," Hendler explains. "Also, I had a strong background in a substantive area, the insurance field, where there were a lot of disputes. The insurance industry is built on fighting claims and settling other claims. I knew hundreds of people who had respect for me because of my professionalism and my evenhandedness. When I said, 'There's this thing called mediation . . . ,' they gave me a try. It's getting the first case that's difficult!"

You can become super successful without having to enter a whole new field of expertise. In fact, the best thing you can do for yourself is build on what you know.

Michael Landrum came to mediation from a solid career working in-house for several Fortune 500 corporations and as a private practice litigator. "I began my professional life as a management-side labor lawyer negotiating union contracts," he says. "Part of my training was to avoid having someone else make the decision. So I always worked at trying to settle things. I like seeing that there are two sides to every story. Rarely, especially in a business dispute, is everybody all right or all wrong.

"What is fun to me," says Landrum, "is the creative effort to try to help people reconcile competing and conflicting interests in a way acceptable to both of them, rather than just attempting to predict who's going to win and why. In civil litigation, if one side is 51 percent more believable, they win. Which means that 49 percent

One Thing Leads to Another

My background is in child welfare and psychotherapy. Back in 1977–78, when I was running a residential treatment center for children in Boulder, I participated in demonstrations against the Rocky Flats Nuclear Weapons facility near Boulder. I met someone who pointed me toward a training of people in nonviolence, and there I met my soon-to-be business partner, Chris Moore. We hit it off and started doing nonviolent peacekeeping and conflict resolution training.

Chris was asked to provide mediation training and asked me to help. I thought this was an interesting way of bringing together my professional and social change interests.

Eventually, four of us decided to quit our day jobs and do this full time. We started CDR Associates, a nonprofit conflict resolution agency, and I've been a partner there for twenty-five years.

When CDR first started we did small community-based cases—small neighborhood disputes, conflicts over noise between fraternities and the university, and so forth. We started a family mediation program and started offering family mediation trainings. Then I got interested in applying mediation to child protection, which became the basis for my doctoral work. And then we realized that we wanted to do more—organizational disputes, public policy mediation, labor-management work. Then we started doing international work—helping other countries develop their own conflict resolution capacity.

Bernie Mayer

of what happened doesn't count. The people who are in the mediation actually solve the problem."

The best thing you can bring to your mediation career is what you already know. If you were a social worker or therapist, you undoubtedly learned skills relating to gaining insight and handling people in emotional situations, and you may have a lot of insight into divorce, health issues, sexual harassment, collaborating to achieve goals, and coming up with creative solutions. Even if you were a lawyer who disliked litigating, you developed some sort of expertise as a litigator—in employment disputes, health issues, labor law, or intellectual property. Whatever your experience has been, value it: it's the foundation you will build on to make yourself visible and viable in the overpopulated mediation market.

Create Your Own Market

Years ago, I had a friend who was an advertising executive. His angle on promoting a service or product was *positioning:* you've got to position the product. Well, as a mediator, *you're* the product. According to my friend's theory, that means you should position yourself in the mediation market. I think a better approach is to *choose* your position in the market according to your real expertise.

For example, if you've been in labor law for years, people in the workplace dispute area know you, and you know them; you're in a natural place to position yourself as a specialist in mediating employment disputes. In a world of commercial mediators, you stand out to clients looking for an employment dispute mediator. I didn't put myself out as a general commercial mediator. I knew I wanted employment cases, so I said, "I do employment law."

The rookie mistake is to try to be all things to all people. If you say, "I mediate litigated cases," what does that really mean? This statement is so general that it doesn't leave footprints in wet sand. When you choose a position—"I choose to mediate intellectual property cases [or employment cases or family law cases]"—you are

You Can't Be All Things to All People

You can't be all things to all people. In an increasingly sophisticated mediation market, the lawyers who are hiring you are going to have their preferences, and they look for a good mix of chemistry, trust, and communication.

Rick Weiler

making a statement people can remember and hang on to. And when you make that statement to the right people, they'll remember you when the time comes.

Find a Gap and Fill It

I learned early on that if you can fill a gap in the marketplace, people will find you. At the beginning of my career, I was able to fill a large gap by helping create a market for mediation. Companies wanted to save court costs, they weren't doing it through the traditional menu offered in court, and I and other pioneers were able to fill that gap by creating the mediation outlet. That opportunity is long gone, but you still have the opportunity to find a gap that's ready to be filled.

Find specific niche areas that haven't been exploited and make them your own. For example, I encouraged my associate to develop expertise in cases concerning the Employment Retirement Income Security Act (ERISA), the federal law governing employment benefits (which includes retirement, disability, health, welfare, and other employment-related benefits), and intellectual property; ERISA is an up-and-coming area, and my associate can get in on the ground floor.

DEVELOP YOUR SKILLS

Sometimes new mediators think of mediation as an offshoot of whatever it was they were doing before. The very best mediators know better. "It's a mind-shift," explains Nina Meierding. "Mediation is not an adjunct of law or therapy, it's a distinct profession. You have to treat it as something unique you have to learn about, not as a given because you're 'good with people.' You have to be willing to go to school, intern, do work to learn new skills. The baseline is having respect for it as a separate profession. Sometimes people go to a forty-hour course and expect to emerge as a full-time mediator. No. Be prepared to invest in time, classes, meeting people, changing your office to look like a mediation office. Think about how many years of *not* making money you are willing to put in."

Basic Training

It's hard to believe that in little more than a decade and a half, the number of professional trainings for mediators has gone from near zero to what seems like a new one every minute: basic mediation training, divorce mediation training, conflict resolution training, collaborative law training, negotiation training, cross-cultural training, advocacy training, advanced mediation training. Trainings are offered by organizations, colleges, and individuals. You can be trained in person, by audio, by video . . . Should you do it? Yes. Why? Because it's important to begin thinking of yourself as a professional from the beginning, and that means doing whatever you can to improve your abilities in the field. Medicine, law, teaching, social work—these and other professions have continuing education requirements to ensure that professionals stay up to speed on new techniques, knowledge, and discoveries in the field. Until our field imposes these requirements on us, we owe it to the profession to impose them ourselves.

Is one training all you need? Not by a long shot. Training is no substitute for experience and personal drive.

Evolve

Forty hours of training do not a mediator make. If you're an art student, the teacher can teach you about color and light and brushes and strokes. But when it comes time to stand in front of the canvas and paint, no one can teach you that. You've got to get in there and evolve your own art. Mediation is a dynamic process. The way I do mediation today isn't even the same as the way I did it last year. Mediation is always evolving. So continuing education is critical.

Robert A. Creo

"Most people start with a forty-hour training course," says Cliff Hendler. "Take the training. Just because you think you've been mediating all your life with family or coworkers doesn't mean you've got the skill set you need to be a professional mediator. The training gives you a framework and understanding of what you're doing and why you're doing it. I've taken hundreds of hours of advanced training in mediation and negotiations. But," he continues, "training only gives you the building blocks you use to build your own style. Think of it this way: you learn the alphabet in school, but your handwriting style is your own." And good handwriting only develops over time, with care and practice.

Beyond Basic Training

Mel, a senior attorney who had basically retired from trial law and decided he was not yet ready to retire altogether, decided that he wanted to learn what this mediation business was all about, and signed up for a six-day course from me. He really enjoyed it and began taking other courses that I taught over the years. Finally, I noticed he had signed up for a course he had taken some years ago, so I gave him a call.

"Mel," I said, "maybe you should take another course—some of my stories might seem stale." He said candidly that he had forgotten the punch lines of most of the stories and wanted to remind himself. "I learned so much the first time," he added, "and enjoyed it so much that I don't mind revisiting the same lessons again."

If you've already had your forty hours and you're a working mediator, continuing education is a must. Many successful mediators provide trainings as part of their product, but that doesn't mean they've learned all they need to know. I learn something new from every mediation I do, from every class I teach to other mediators, and from books. I read books on mediation, of course, but I also read books on social psychology, negotiation, influence, and leadership, as well as other books, including novels, that have nothing to do with mediation at all. And I take away a valuable gem from almost every one. I know I'm not alone in this. "I'm always reading new business books, medical books, and textbooks as they come out," says one mediator, "because I want to keep up with how ideas are developing. I get my ideas by being inspired by other people."

You never know where you'll find your next great insight into your work. Several years ago, I even got new insights into mediation from my participation in a stand-up comedy class—a place where I had never expected to find similarities at all. But as it turned out, the similarities between stand-up comedy and mediation are remarkable. Among other things, I discovered that the emotional association a comedian has with an audience is the same as the one a mediator has with the disputants. A comedian who ignores the temperature in the room and simply recites memorized jokes is going to bomb. A mediator who follows the basic format taught in Mediation 101 and who doesn't consider the individual quirks and concerns of the specific parties in a negotiation is never going to connect with them.

If you are new to the field, consider finding a mentor. (We'll talk more about this in Chapter Five.) At the very least, ask mediators you admire if you can observe them at work. Many students from Pepperdine Law School have shadowed me over the years. Their questions and feedback about the process put me more in touch with what I am trying to accomplish for the parties. They make me think twice about my approaches and encourage me to use good judgment. Aside from that, clients seem to get a kick out of having an observer present. They feel almost honored.

IT'S YOUR CALLING

"Mediation is my personal journey," says Michelle Obradovic. "I was born to it. I don't feel like I ever had a choice but to do what I do. It's me putting myself out there, completely open, and trying to help people be the best they can be." It should now be abundantly clear that for top-tier mediators, mediation is far more than a career: it's a lifestyle and a calling, and everything in our life speaks to it.

"Get training and continually train, read, and work on practicing skills, even if you are not mediating much," advises Susan Hammer. "The great thing is you can use mediation skills in everyday life whenever there's a difference in point of view. Practice what you're preaching all the time to get it ground into you. It will become part of you, a way of life. This will make you more credible; you will start to carry yourself as a mediator, to think and speak as one."

TOP-TIER STRATEGIES

1. Be yourself.

There are literally thousands of mediators in the market, and more are coming up every day. But there's only one you. It's your unique background, talents, skills, and personal strengths that people will be drawn to. Let them see the real you in every encounter. Don't try to drive the ball like Tiger Woods if you don't have the club head speed.

2. Practice authenticity.

Your authenticity is rooted in your commitment to truth and to getting the best settlement possible for all parties, and in your absolute willingness to see the process through to the end. When you are working from a place of authenticity, people feel—rightly—that you are doing your best for them from the best possible intentions. In turn, they will be motivated to stick with you and return again and again.

3. Create your own market.

Jumping into what looks like the most lucrative field simply because that's where the money is, is probably the worst thing you can do for your career. Build your own market out of your own interests and expertise, and people will seek you out for exactly what you're best at.

4. Learn from everything.

Forty hours of training is a start, but don't stop there. The best and most successful mediators are always learning— from classes, trainings, and seminars; from conversations and online chats with colleagues; from reading and absorbing everything they can get their hands on; and from every mediation they do. Be a shark: never stop swimming.

3

Invisible Marketing
The Essence of Networking

*The most effective marketing is doing your best on
a case.*

Rick Weiler

Two lawyers meet over a game of golf on a Saturday afternoon: "I've got a potentially nasty malpractice suit that really needs to settle out of court. Do you know any mediators who can handle it?"

"I've used Ted on a couple of real bears. One of the parties actually walked out in the middle of negotiations, and Ted managed to reel him back in without breaking a sweat."

"Yeah, I've heard he really sticks with a case until it settles. Fran told me he worked magic for her more than once. But he charges a fortune, doesn't he?"

"You get what you pay for. What difference does it make, particularly if the case settles?"

"Say no more. I'll give him a call this afternoon."

Closing cases—having a reputation as a mediator who gets things done—really is the most effective marketing you can do. Next to great negotiation skills, this "invisible" marketing—when word about your prowess as a mediator gets out and you're suddenly on everyone's radar—is what powers some people to the top. For those who are natural-born salespeople, knowing how this kind of

Keeping Clients Happy

Marketing is a process, not an event. It happens all the time: while you're mediating the case and in everything you do. At base, it's the process of creating frontal lobe awareness: when the customer is ready to buy, they think of you.

Studies done by bar associations prove over and over again that lawyers get more business from existing clients than from new clients. So you have to keep existing clients happy while you slowly but surely acquire new clients. The goal in business terms is to keep the customers happy and coming back. So, from a business point of view, keeping the customers—the lawyers, not the parties—happy is more important than jamming through a settlement. If you settle a case and the lawyers aren't happy, they won't be back.

Ralph Williams

networking works is intuitive. For the rest of us, fortunately, it's a skill we can work on and learn.

GIVE PEOPLE A STORY TO TELL ABOUT YOU

In his best-seller *Blink*, Malcolm Gladwell writes about how we unconsciously absorb impressions and make decisions in the blink of an eye—and tend to stick with these decisions despite information that might prove them wrong. Uncomfortable as it may be for us to contemplate, people select mediators in the same way. They generally don't engage in weeks and months of research, collecting

Invisible Marketing   55

and collating pages of data. Instead of using hard facts, they often base their decision on intangibles—your reputation as a closer, the personal impression you make, your "buzz." As Rod Max says, "It begins before you start. If you don't have a reputation for trust, fair judgment, the knowledge of the process, you're not going to get anywhere. Some big companies hire dozens of mediators, but the truth is that mediation is a personalized thing: 'I want Rod Max, not Joe Schmo.'"

If you give people a great story to tell about you, your reputation not only precedes you but markets you. Better yet, have someone else provide the comment or story line about you, and use it in your profile. A great employment lawyer once described me as "tenacious as a German shepherd with a steak." I consider that one of the best compliments I've ever had—and it makes a great story line for people to tell about me. I'm not the only mediator who sticks with a case until it settles—far from it, in fact—but this colorful epithet is a lot more fun for people to recall than "tenacious."

What stories do you know—or tell—about the superstars in our field? No doubt you've heard about the guy whose career is in the stratosphere. He charges five figures per diem, wins multimillion-dollar settlements regularly, and has houses all over the world. He may really be the greatest mediator of all time, or he may not be doing anything in the mediation room that you wouldn't do. But he's got the buzz, and people clamor to do business with him.

In this sense, he has much in common with other popular products. A lot of people want the latest-model iPod, whether or not they already have a thousand songs on their computer. They also want that BlackBerry hanging off their belt, even though they don't travel, make a lot of calls, or send much email. And they've got to have that super-fast computer because they're sure it will make them do their work better. Whether we're talking iPods or mediators, everybody wants what everybody else is buying—and never mind the cost. In fact, some clients feel that paying higher fees means they're getting the top of the line. They just gotta have it. One top mediator puts it bluntly: "When you get to some level of these cases, to pay the mediator $100,000 is a drop in the bucket. If people are concerned about my fee, then (1) their case does not have much value, and (2) they're not looking for a process that deserves my expertise."

Compelling, positive stories about you and your work can and will create a steady stream of clients fighting to get on your calendar. It's all about reaching critical mass, or—to borrow another phrase from Gladwell—finding your personal tipping point. As Geoff Sharp says, "Word of mouth is *the* way work comes in the door."

Stories come from life experience. Get involved with people and communities that are of interest to you and can potentially be sources of business, such as bar associations or human resources organizations or whatever communities form your interest area. Listen to what people have to say, and incorporate their needs into your repertoire. Share your stories with them, and they will share them with others. Be an author—write articles that say interesting things in an interesting way and let other people quote you. Author an article that appears on a conflict resolution Web site. Volunteer as a committee member in your local trade associations. Become involved in a case that has international dimensions. These are all things you end up putting in your biography, and they put meat on the bones of your story as you do them. Set a list of five things you can do in the upcoming year that will get your name in lights. They don't have to be huge projects, but in some small way they should serve to make your name more visible to prospective clients.

Here's an added bonus: you are creating paths that lead to people you haven't met and things you haven't thought about yet. If you volunteer to be on the courts committee, for example, you will meet leaders of all the bar associations and the judges who will be consulting with you on how to make the court system better. The person you talked to on the trial bar may be pitching you right now as a high-profile mediator—just because you got involved. All of a sudden, you have become a resource in the community and have elevated your status almost effortlessly.

The Four R's

Remember the three R's? My approach is sort of the four R's: Results that lead to Reputation that lead to Referrals that lead to Repeat business.

Paul Monicatti

THE MEDIATION TIPPING POINT

"People are interested in outcome," says Robert Jenks. "If you never settle a case, you're not going to get used a lot." Sometimes, all it takes is settling the *right* case.

Some years ago, a mediator friend of mine who had been toiling in the middle tier of the pyramid for some years had one big miracle malpractice case that he pulled out of the fire. The plaintiff and defendant had been in litigation literally for years, and the animosity was thick. They had agreed to mediation as a last-ditch measure, but no one held out much hope for success. But my friend worked the case and did the impossible: not only did the parties settle but tears flowed, recriminations ceased, apologies ensued, and money changed hands. In short, he did his job and did it well—just as he'd been doing for years. The two attorneys, however, were wildly impressed. They started using him regularly rather than going straight to litigation. And they sang his praises to anyone who would listen, calling him the "miracle man." That was the tipping point for him. Before he knew it, his calendar was filled, and it has stayed filled to this day.

Another friend dedicated six weeks to resolving a multiparty construction defect case. She stayed on the phone with dozens of lawyers every day, until all the pieces of the puzzle were put together.

The Way to Get Business Is to Mediate Well

I believe that good mediators don't have time to meet and greet. The way to get business is to mediate well. I'll start mediating at 7:30 A.M., and it may be midnight until we have the direction. It may get resolved at 2 A.M. Then you've got to follow up to conclude all terms. If you're mediating three days a week, the other two days you're designing and following up. It may be that I've got to get on the phone with the parties after we've already met—I'm the first person on their mind. The bottom line is not my advertising; it's the work I do.

Rod Max

In the process, she developed a relationship with each attorney, and her dedication and tenacity were impossible to miss. She ended up receiving referrals from every lawyer on that case, and it launched her practice.

Los Angeles mediator Ralph Williams advises, "Fish where the fish are." And that's good advice. But you don't have to catch all the fish in the sea; you just have to catch a couple of live ones. As my friends' experience illustrates, lawyers multiply exponentially. A handful of satisfied clients who like you on one case will each use you on another case, where you'll meet more lawyers who'll use you on other cases, where you'll meet more lawyers! As Susan Hammer says in something of an understatement, "Every contact you make in the bar potentially leads to something. I've had lots of good relationships with an awful lot of people. No matter what ads you run, word of mouth is what helps you ultimately."

FIRST IMPRESSIONS COUNT

It may seem shallow, but it's almost inevitable: we naturally tend to equate physical attractiveness with such traits as talent, kindness, honesty, and intelligence, and unconsciously assume that attractive people possess these traits. Perhaps because of this, people who are perceived as attractive are generally more persuasive at getting what they want and changing others' attitudes. Interestingly, among successful mediators, few would be mistaken for models or movie stars. Most of us are just regular people who have this in common: we know how to make a great first impression. Understanding the importance of putting your best foot forward, and knowing how to do it, can take you a long way.

Would John Wayne Negotiate?

Why do so few people actually go to mediators first? Why do they think they need to go to lawyers first?

Would John Wayne negotiate? No. That's our basic culture. John Wayne is not just a movie star; he is an icon—he is what many Americans say they want to be. He is the incarnation of the statement, "You should come back with your shield or on it." Only the weak negotiate. So most people feel that they've got to have a lawyer to protect them. They don't trust themselves or like to negotiate, and want to leave it to the lawyer. The marketing task is to let people know that negotiation does not require selling out or compromising.

Robert Benjamin

It is vital to make a phenomenal impression—not just a "good" impression—at every point of contact with clients or potential clients. That means looking your best, dressing your best, presenting the best genuine "you" possible. But you need to deliver a one-two punch: package yourself well *and* follow up with the glow of your genuine interest and intelligence. If people like what they see and you welcome them sincerely, they'll take time to discover what else you have to offer.

LAWYERS ARE THE GATEKEEPERS

Unless you're working in public policy or in another area of mediation where lawyers are less present in the process, the most direct route to clients is through their lawyers. Lawyers are the gatekeepers of mediation. Everyone says this, and everyone is right.

"Most people call a lawyer if they are worried and want the problem solved—especially in the business world," says Cliff Hendler. "Businesspeople virtually *never* call their mediator. And the lawyers go to the mediators because lawyers want to manage their risk. Ninety-nine percent of lawyers don't want to go to court. It's risky and costly, and most know that they'll do much, much better in negotiated resolutions than in trial."

"Mediators often underestimate the importance of being known to the gatekeepers of conflict (often lawyers in my world)," says Geoff Sharp. "We are not like other professions, as we are not interchangeable. That is why it is hard to leverage mediation practice—the gatekeepers use me because I am me, and go to Joe down the road because he is him."

Think about it: almost regardless of your specialty and client base, lawyers hold the keys to the cases you want on your calendar. They're the ones who know and choose the mediators. Of course, mediators who have made it to the top of the pyramid generally do not have to hustle to find cases. By the time they've reached the

Other Gatekeepers

One reason lawyers are successful is that they work within the primary system developed for dealing with conflict in our society. Lawyers are the gatekeepers for a lot of conflicts that pay for mediation. But the legal network is not the only way to get business. Public policy mediation is usually funded through government agencies. The health and mental health communities are often referral sources. Direct connection to people actually in the disputes is another way. For people starting out, working for a conflict resolution organization is a good way to make contacts.

Bernie Mayer

stratosphere, cases find them. But no one has a lock on the top, so for most of us, client development is an ongoing process—and, truth be told, one we tend to enjoy.

"Marketing is an interesting proposition for us mediators who are within the legal community," says Sharp. "Marketing is not something that lawyers easily accept, either when they do it themselves to clients or when it is done to them. I think a mediator in the legal world needs to be understated about marketing and remember they are still working within the legal environment. Providing value and content is the key: marketing with something in it for the recipient."

Los Angeles mediator Jeff Kichaven agrees. "I try to communicate to my client community—other lawyers—that I remain concerned about what they do and what their troubles and worries are.

I don't present myself as someone trying to sell them something, but as someone who is trying to help them with their problem and who understands what their world is about."

In the more visible kind of marketing we'll talk about in the next chapter, always remember this vital community. Speak to their groups, write articles for their journals, keep up on legal news, attend their events, and consider their interests. Lawyers not only want a reasonable outcome but need to look good in front of their clients. When you make that happen for them, they're yours for life.

SHARED SIMILARITIES
CREATE CONNECTIONS

"You have a dog too? No kidding. I love my dog. We'll have to get them together some afternoon." Is it that easy? Sometimes.

We tend to enjoy the company of people who are similar to us or who feel somehow familiar—whether in our opinions, personality traits, background, or lifestyle. This doesn't mean that you have to repeatedly clone yourself to match every potential client. Rather, you can draw from your authenticity to try to find some connection that you share with the other person.

I give my clients every opportunity to connect with me as soon as they walk into my mediation center. Their eyes may be drawn to the 1956 Sandy Koufax baseball card on the wall or to a bookshelf full of really interesting books or to a unique display of materials connected to my father's 1959 patent for a machine that automated the installation of draperies—and, of course, I'm happy to talk to them about any or all of these, because each reflects something I enjoy. "You like baseball? So do I!" I find that something in the array of memorabilia in my office is bound to appeal to someone, and inevitably this creates a sense of connection.

Similarities, no matter how small, give the other person an additional reason to buy into what you're selling—be it why mediation is better than litigation in this case, why the case is worth what you say it is, or even why your fee is reasonable. For example, you've already had a very pleasant conversation with a new client about your golden retrievers, how much you enjoy golf, and the fact that you're shopping for a new Beemer much like the one she owns. As simplistic as this may sound, you've created common ground between you. Now your new client is thinking, "Hey, we're not all that different—maybe his point of view isn't as far-fetched as I thought it was."

INCREASE FAMILIARITY THROUGH REPEATED CONTACT

Your familiar presence at meetings, your brief phone calls to say thanks or check in on the progress of a case or just touch base . . . top mediators understand intuitively that increased familiarity through repeated contact with people tends to increase your appeal, making your success in mediation and in client development more likely. "I do a lot of premediation contact," says Michael Landrum. "Phone calls, 'house calls' to meet with the lawyers in their offices days or a week or two before the mediation. They like that because it's not in the throes of battle during the mediation, when tension is high."

"When a case is over," says Robert A. Creo, "whether it settles or not, face-to-face contact is good. Engaging in a dialogue with the lawyers is good. Some people send thank-you notes."

If you begin a mediation with lawyers you've spoken with only once, over the phone, they may not feel familiar enough with you to be receptive to your ideas. It's hard to talk dollars to settle the case with someone who feels like a stranger. You are much more likely to be persuasive on every level if you have reached out and made personal, face-to-face contact with the parties well before the negotiation. Repeated contact on neutral ground puts all of you at ease, leading the way to a more productive and profitable negotiation and future work together.

SOLVE THEIR PROBLEM

My formula for networking is somewhat counterintuitive. When you meet people who might be useful in helping you get new clients, the *last* thing you should do is tell them about your mediation practice. Instead, follow the same advice dating mavens gave to teenage girls in the 1950s: ask them questions about themselves. In fact, creating relationships is all about asking questions. And you have to offer a swap: learn what their problem is and offer to help them out of it.

One day, for example, over a long business lunch, I noticed that my friend, normally an easygoing guy, was drumming his fingers on the table. I asked, "What's up, Mike? You seem tense."

"I've got some cases pending that are threatening to sink the ship," he said. "If I lose these cases, that's it—I might as well just kiss my firm good-bye and go look for another line of work." He downed what was left of his drink and started looking around for the waiter.

"I'm really sorry to hear that," I said. "Do you think any of your clients might be open to mediation? Settling those cases instead of litigating them might get you out of the rough."

"I don't know, Jeff," he replied. "Maybe."

"Well, who are the opposing attorneys? Maybe I have some history with them that we could play off here to turn this thing around."

He looked up. "Could you really do that? I know your calendar's probably jammed up."

"Let me see what I can do, Mike," I said. "I'd like to see you get out of this mess alive."

In my experience, people will buy mediation services only if they have a problem that needs fixing. Discovering and addressing what potential clients need is the most direct route to client development. Mike eventually brought me those cases. The key to closing the deal was in my knowing that what he really needed was someone to sympathize with his predicament, understanding that mediation offered a clean way out of the problem, and assuring him that I would be able to take care of the problem.

"What Can I Do to Help?"

For me, the client-mediator relationship is based on a helping paradigm: attorneys are in pain because, as was true for my friend Mike, losing a particular case threatens their career. Parties are in pain for a multiplicity of reasons: their business is in trouble, they're going to lose everything in a divorce, they've suffered at the hands of the health care system and someone is going to pay, they were screwed over by their employer and want what's coming to them, they lost a child to a drunk driver—and they want to be reassured that I can make that pain better by somehow evening the score. They don't want to know *how* I'm going to do it; they just want to believe that I've done it many times before and can do it for them.

Like a doctor making a diagnosis, I ask questions, probing gently, trying to find the source of their pain. When they see that I really do understand their problem and care about seeing that it gets solved, it's only a few short steps to getting their case on my calendar.

Show That You Care

"Why do I keep having this nightmare, Doc?"

"Why don't you tell me why *you* think you're having that nightmare?"

If you've ever read a cartoon about a psychiatrist, you're familiar with the technique called reversing: answering a question with a question. When a client calls with a potential case and asks, "Have you ever handled a case involving a widget manufacturer?" I never say no. Most cases, as we all know, are not really about widgets or improper surgical techniques or malicious spouses. Invariably, something deeper is at work, and that's the level on which we operate in a mediation. So instead of answering the potential clients' questions directly—and perhaps inadvertently inviting them to look elsewhere—I focus on engaging them. So I respond with a question: "Why don't you tell me more about the case. What's going on?"

I'm trying to diagnose their condition, so right away I want to learn more about the conflict and what's driving it, and the whole time I'm positioning myself as a professional. Because honestly, it *doesn't* matter if I've never handled a case exactly like the one they've got. What they really want to know is whether I can get them out of a painful situation.

If you try to sell yourself by talking at length about all the cases you've settled in the past, you're probably going to lose a substantial number of clients you might have had. But if you let them do the talking—and if you truly listen and respond to what they are saying—they will feel your concern and respond in turn. By the end of the conversation, they will see that you understand their problem, and you will already have begun building the reservoir of trust you can draw from as the case goes forward.

CREATING VALUE

Whether I'm actively negotiating or in premediation sessions, I'm always working to provide direction and encouragement, giving clients new tools for solving problems, guiding them around potential land mines, and trying to create new opportunities. I think of this as creating value.

In fact, creating value might well be the foundation for getting clients and settling cases. The main focus is on providing leadership to parties so that they don't walk into the minefields that brought them into the dispute. When marketing your services, you can create value by finding out from the parties what their pain threshold is, what's causing them the most concern, and what has to happen in order for them to select you as the person who can help them solve their problem. Once you have this information, you can innovate regarding how to solve their problem.

Let potential clients know what's in it for them. For example, a client once told me that he'd like to use me on a big case, but felt that the defense might view me as too expensive. So he figured he would suggest three less costly garden-variety retired judges as mediators. But he didn't have a lot of confidence in these guys, and he was afraid the case would end up in court—and if that happened, his job was on the line. Like most people in this kind of pain, he gave up some important information: he was in deep trouble. The case had to get settled. Armed with that information, I knew I was already halfway to closing the deal.

I reminded him that if the defense agreed to use me at the "exorbitant" rates I charge, that might actually serve as a signal to the plaintiff lawyer that the defense was serious about his case and that they might come to the table in a manner he would find appealing. You could see the wheels turning in the client's mind. Once he saw the situation in this light, he was easily able to convince the other side to select me as the mediator.

When clients are concerned that they have a bet-the-firm kind of case, why would they go to you? Because they trust you to resolve the case successfully. So if you intend to charge high-end fees for your services, you've got to be a bet-the-firm kind of mediator—somebody who is willing to stand up and get the job done in a complex civil action, no matter how long it takes. Clients need to know that what you do best is pull their fat out of the fire. I always tell them, "When it looks like the deal is going south, that's when I do my best work." When it looks like there's no hope for a case, I can get creative, finding options and surprising ways to make things work.

Inspiration is great when it happens, but you can't truthfully tell clients that inspiration always strikes when you most need it! Beneath inspiration, then, is what every mediator is really selling: hope. Your mantra needs to go something like this: I'm the person you need when things are falling apart around you, when you need somebody to pick up the pieces and get the job on track. Of course, you always have to back up that claim with results.

CLOSING THE DEAL

Ralph Williams puts his marketing philosophy simply: "We don't sell mediation services; we sell closed cases." And that's a key point. People are willing to invest money in settling a case. Because my fees are on the high end of the spectrum, most clients seek me out only when they're ready to settle. If they are willing to make this investment in my time, then even before the case begins, I know it's going settle.

Practically speaking, before you close the deal and decide to put a new case on your calendar, make sure the client has the budget for it. You may be in the mediation business because you love it— and I hope you are—but if you're going to make money as a mediator, you have to make sure your clients are prepared to pay serious money for your services. If they're not, well, you may not be the right mediator for them at this time.

If they do have the budget and you feel you can settle their case, then closing the deal is like the last hand in a high-stakes poker game.

"I know you can do the job, but I'm not sure my client will spring for it," more than one client has told me. "There are a lot of good mediators out there who charge a lot less."

"It's up to you," I respond, "but think of it this way: you can go with a cheaper mediator, or you can spend more—and the other party's lawyer will pick up the other half. You'll get a great mediator *and* a message from the other side that they're all in. They're not going to spend all that money for a day's work and not settle at the end of the day."

And what if we *don't* settle at the end of the day? Well, when that happens, I say, "Come back later, and we'll finish up—no charge." And I stick with the case, by telephone and remediation if necessary, until it settles. The clients appreciate it, and it becomes another part of the story they tell about me.

Elevator Talk

I am amazed that, without knowing a scintilla of mediation theory, parties often reflect in the elevator on the way down from the mediation. And what they say could be lifted straight from a mediation textbook. In fact, I really do ask the lawyers what their client said in the elevator as one of the questions in my feedback form!

Geoff Sharp

REFERRING BUSINESS TO OTHER MEDIATORS

"I want to thank you for recommending Jack to mediate that employment case for me last month," said Ann, a lawyer I've known for years. "When you told me your schedule was full, I panicked. I know I can count on you to make sure everyone gets a fair shake in a negotiation, so I had some trepidation about going into this thing with a new face. But he was terrific—he gained our trust immediately. Even the plaintiff's attorney liked him."

"That's great to hear," I replied. And I meant it.

"Don't worry," she smiled. "You're still our top choice."

I was glad to hear I was her top choice, but I was equally glad that she liked my referral. If you're successful, you'll have a lot of days when your calendar is so full you actually have to turn people away. In this enviable situation, you've got to be confident enough to make referrals to other top mediators and be willing to let go of the client.

Don't be afraid to collaborate. Referring successful mediators will result in exponential referrals because these mediators will refer their clients back to you. I offer two caveats, however. First, make sure the mediators you refer are willing to collaborate. Referrals to people who want to hold on to clients as though they own them will backfire. Second, the mediators you refer have to be great closers; don't refer anybody who can't get the job done. Always make sure that the mediator you recommend is up to the challenge, because his or her inability to settle a dispute may reflect on you.

Referring mediators you trust can actually be a good source of referrals for *you*. Whenever I've given someone else's name, the client always agrees with my recommendation—it's like a closed deal because they trust me. And that mediator then feels free to refer a case to me.

EMBRACE REJECTION

When the lawyer in the previous story said I was still her "top choice," I was flattered—but my response was well tempered by reality. I know that no matter how hard I try, I'll never get everybody's vote. Mediation is an isolated world. For every case you get, there are ten you didn't. And you're only selected after others are rejected. It's important to recognize that in this field, every new case is a beauty contest, and people tend to be very discriminating about whom they choose as the winner.

To be really successful you have to expect rejection and embrace it. You must hold the view that when you've been rejected, it means that someone who believes in you has tried to sell you. He or she will keep putting your name out there, and eventually you'll achieve critical mass. I hear the statement "Oh, your name comes up all the time" from people who have never used me.

Don't let rejection get to you. You may be on every lawyer's list of three top mediators, but you've got to remember that there are two other mediators up there with you. You just can't take the deci-

Leave Your Need for Recognition at the Door

The mediation business in most markets is more about what people think or perceive of you as a mediator than who (you may think) you are. It is a high-touch, highly personal business. What you may think of how well you did on a case may be contrary to the subsequent story the participants tell. Mediators are invisible and forgettable, despite the great work and service we deliver. People meet us when they are in conflict. If the conflict resolves, it is no surprise that human nature wants to put it in the past and move on. People desiring to do this work should not expect or need to be revered, rewarded, or recognized. We do it because it is a higher calling, and we earn the right by accepting the unbounded responsibility it requires to be good.

Tracy Allen

sion personally. It may be based on timing or scheduling, or the would-be clients just plain prefer another mediator over you that day.

EXPRESS GRATITUDE

If you show up for mediations with the attitude that you're doing the parties a favor by saving them time and money in litigation, you'd better not expect any repeat business. No matter how big you get, you can never take clients for granted.

I can't tell you how many big-money cases I have had that settled when I succeeded in encouraging one of the parties simply to apologize to the other or to express gratitude in an uncomfortable situation. The same principle applies to developing your client base.

Cast your bread upon the waters, and it will come back to you a thousandfold. Express real gratitude to the attorneys or to the parties to demonstrate that you appreciate their selecting you, and they will come back to you again and again.

"Successful mediators care," says Gary Furlong. "They care about all the parties, and respect the fact that the parties have difficult decisions to make during the process. There are many mediators with good expertise or technical skills, and depending on the style of mediator you are, those are the price of admission. But caring, really caring, sets successful mediators apart."

Robert Jenks says, "After the mediation I always thank the people I worked with. 'I was honored; it was a pleasure to work with you.' This is an important key to building a successful practice."

First—and last—impressions count! No matter how good the outcome of mediation is, people will initially base their decision to hire you on the first, and they'll keep hiring you based on the last. That's why a simple thank-you at the end of the process is so important.

"When you can sincerely say, at the end of a mediation, 'Thank you for giving me the opportunity to be part of your life, your situation. I'm pleased we got this done today. I hope you got some closure and you can move on,' this kind of humanity becomes part of your marketing," reflects Robert A. Creo. "It comes across to the participants. But it has to be sincere. You have to feel it."

Some mediators make phone calls to participants, others send thank-you notes. The form is flexible, but it is the sincerity that people remember. From time to time I send clients a personalized email cartoon, a quick creative acknowledgment and thank-you for their participation. Other times I might drop a note or email to one or more of the participants thanking them for their professionalism in the way they handled the case. The most successful mediators make expressing gratitude part of their daily activities—not because they are manipulative sons of bitches but because they are truly grateful to be able to do this kind of work and get paid real money for doing it! When you derive real satisfaction from your work, people see it and want to hire you again.

TOP-TIER STRATEGIES

1. Give people a story to tell about you.

When it comes to setting yourself apart from the competition, word of mouth is everything—buzz counts. Never underestimate the power of making yourself an interesting character in your own story. Empower other people to be the champion of your story by giving them something of value to talk about: mediate well, demonstrate your expertise in articles or talks, join organizations in your community of potential clients, and share ideas with the people you most need to know.

2. Make a good first impression.

This advice isn't just for prom dates; it's crucial for mediators. In our profession we are selling ourselves. People will not want to spend hours in a negotiation with a person who doesn't seem to fit in with the group, and they will make that snap judgment the first time they meet you. You never know when you're going to make the acquaintance of your next important client. Make the effort to look your best and project your most professional self at every opportunity.

3. Remember that lawyers are the gatekeepers of mediation.

Unless you are working in the area of government and public policy, the vast majority of your cases will come through the kindness of lawyers. Lawyers are the gate-keepers of mediation, and lawyers—not their parties—are your clients. Do everything possible to ensure that you create and keep a good rapport with them: join their organizations, read their journals, become friends with them.

4. Build relationships through increased familiarity and frequency of contact.

We all want to spend time with people who feel familiar and with whom we share common interests or points of view. Your clients are no different! Encourage connections by sharing your own interests, and do everything you can to be a familiar and welcome face or voice on the phone.

5. Create value whenever possible.

In mediation, the main focus of value creation is on leading the parties around the minefields that brought them into the dispute. When marketing your services, you can create value by helping clients find a way out of whatever pain they are in that brought them to you in the first place—a rancorous and complicated case that seems impossible to resolve, a case that will cripple the law firm if it doesn't settle, and so on. When they see you as the person who can bring them out of this darkness and into the light—and you are able to back up that perception with good work—you have created value for all concerned. You're not selling yourself; you're selling your ability to solve the problem.

6. Remember that you're selling closed deals.

Clients would not be coming to you if going to court was their first option. That means they are looking to you to be a closer—to settle the case amicably and fairly. But before you can do that, you have to close the deal that involves selecting you as their mediator. Think of it as a high-stakes poker game and make sure they're ready to go "all in" with you before you start negotiating. If they're willing to pay your fee and you've got that commitment, you're more than halfway to settling before you've even begun.

7. **Embrace rejection and express gratitude.**

When you don't get a case, you can't take it personally. If you do, you'll be feeling pretty bad most of the time! Accept rejection philosophically and move on. When you settle a case, be sure to express gratitude to the parties for sticking with you to the end, as well as to the attorneys who brought the case to you. A simple thank-you, sincerely expressed, is the right thing to do and a good way to ensure that the clients will remember you favorably next time—and perhaps it will mean a little *less* rejection down the line.

4

Visible Marketing
Getting Out There

A lot of people say, "I want to be a mediator, so I'm gonna go get trained."

Great. Then what?

"Well, then people will call me."

No they won't—not unless you get out there and tell 'em. You can have the best fried chicken in the world. But if you don't have a sign, no one's getting off the interstate to eat it.

Robert Jenks

Highly successful mediators know they're lucky to be where they are. So when the top professionals talk about how they got there, many can't help but give credit to plain good fortune.

"In a word," says Ben Picker, "I consider myself 'lucky.' I have been chairman of a midsized firm, chancellor (Philadelphia's word for president) of the 15,000-member Philadelphia Bar Association, and have served in leadership positions in numerous other civic and professional associations. I have always written and lectured in my areas of expertise. As a consequence, I was well known and well respected as a leader in my profession and in the community even before I embarked on my mediation career."

Paul Monicatti also says, "I've been lucky. I was lucky enough to get in on the mediation profession early and be in the right place at the right time. I haven't had to do much advertising or marketing."

I, too, have said many times that I was in the right place at the right time, lucky to get in on the ground floor of an exciting new area of practice. Yet no matter how lucky we are or how successful we've been in the conference room and caucus room, we've all learned that we have to go the extra mile to make ourselves visible: doing whatever we can to get our names and faces and bodies out there where clients and potential clients can see us, hear us, and get to know us one-on-one. We can't always count on the equation *raw talent + settled cases + sheer good luck = career success* in a field as crowded as mediation has become. In such markets as Los Angeles, Toronto, Texas, Florida, and a few others, if you don't add *effective marketing* to the equation, you're sabotaging your potential success.

Bernie Mayer puts the marketing task succinctly: "Do follow-ups. Train. Consult. Teach. Write. Don't just mediate."

Ben Picker agrees. "I often tell individuals who have the training and are ready to start a mediation practice that marketing is not a sport for the short winded. In order to succeed, you must make the same commitment to marketing that you hopefully have made over the years for important projects on behalf of yourself or your clients.

"The choices you can make are highly individualized," Picker continues, "and you should make choices consistent with your own personality. Writing? Training? Teaching? Networking? Advertising? Joining with other professionals? All of the above? Other activities? Again, these choices depend on your personality and strengths and also will vary from region to region. All of these efforts will take time. In order to succeed, you must be both persistent and patient."

Michigan's Tracy Allen describes just how much time these efforts take. "Initially, my fifteen-year reputation as a lawyer formed the foundation for being able to build a mediation practice. I invested (and still do) enormous amounts of capital in building my practice—then and now—and it is *time. My time.* I have written, spoken, networked, lectured, volunteered, et cetera, thousands of hours in ADR [alternative dispute resolution] to establish a knowledge and experience base as an ADR service provider. I have immersed myself in the mediation profession."

Seasonal Marketing

There are times of the year when certain types of work come more often. In Canada, it's cold! When it starts to get warm and you can put a shovel in the ground, construction projects begin. So we always send out something around March to our construction partnering clients.

Late August is a good time of year to market to law firms because they're all coming back from vacation.

Rick Russell

It is critical that you devote time to being present with the prospects who might hire you. Being present means actively participating in activities where your clients spend *their* time, not merely showing up and staying out of the action, waiting for something to happen. Be involved with those activities. "I show up everywhere and work the room," says Michelle Obradovic. "I don't go to a cocktail party and sit against the wall!" Even if you're talking to one person all night at a meeting or a dinner, be there for that person as if he or she were the most important person in the world. That one contact could end up being your most important client.

WORKING THE BUTTERFLY EFFECT

You've probably heard of the so-called butterfly effect. The idea grew out of chaos theory and was first popularized in 1962 in a paper by Edward Lorenz titled "Does the Flap of a Butterfly's Wings in Brazil Set Off a Tornado in Texas?" The basic idea is that even though things may seem random, everything is really part of an exceedingly complex but interconnected system in which small

>
>
> ## Motivated by a Passion for Mediation
>
> Motivated by a passion for mediation and my commitment to the process, I began early in my mediation career to write, lecture, train, and network among others in the profession. Interestingly, I was not motivated by any particular desire to build a practice. I simply wanted to learn from others and share my experiences with them. I also enjoyed the collegiality.
>
> *Ben Picker*

changes in behavior can cause large and unforeseen consequences. I feel that the butterfly effect applies to marketing yourself as a mediator: you can never predict the effect of your relatively small efforts—a training, a speaking engagement, or even a conversation at the airport while you're waiting for a plane—but sometimes the gains are surprisingly big.

It's funny, but most of what I have come to see as "marketing myself"—teaching classes, doing speaking engagements, attending meetings of like-minded professionals and getting to know them better—I always considered to be part of the fun of being a mediator. I love getting to know new people, hanging out with old friends and acquaintances, and sharing knowledge with others who love this type of work as much as I do. Much of the time I spend *not* mediating is time spent engaging with others. What, they pay me for this? And I get new work too? Great!

Get in Opportunity's Way

In Arthur Golden's *Memoirs of a Geisha*, the heroine reflects on an accidental yet life-changing meeting: "We lead our lives like water flowing down a hill, going more or less in one direction until we splash into something that forces us to find a new course." We can count on the fact that if we just live our lives, eventually we'll bump into things that send us in one direction or another. Instead of waiting for opportunity to knock, however, I prefer to get in opportunity's way.

That said, I don't mean you should approach opportunity mindlessly, hoping you'll run into something. "You can't focus on your goal until you've defined it," says Robert Jenks, and I agree wholeheartedly.

Before you begin to explore all the ways you can make yourself visible, sit down and think hard about who you really are as a mediator and decide on the market niche you want to target.

Birds of a Feather Flock Together

So many mediators want to (and think they can) field any kind of business that comes their way. They say proudly and loudly, "I mediate everything!" certain that variety is the key to success. But if you're vague about the focus of your practice, where do you go for clients? You've just made the community you're going after enormous—and faceless. Although doing so may seem counterintuitive, you must *reduce* the area in which you're seeking contacts by being more of a specialist. Only then will you find a business arena you can visit and revisit often enough to make an impact.

Think of it this way: birds of a feather flock together. If you're trying to fit into flocks of ostriches, ducks, robins, and flamingos, what are your chances of finding a welcoming wing to usher you into the group?

When you're trying to pinpoint a specialty, start from what you know. "Work with your strength," says Gary Furlong. "If you come from a legal background, cultivate the area of law you know best. If you come from a human resources background, cultivate the organizational field first. Then get the training and experience in the other areas you want to work in before going there as a mediator."

The formula is fairly simple: decide who you'd like your clients to be and then put yourself where they can see you. Study the pool of potential clients. Look for a well-established, cohesive business

Opening Up the Market

I view the mediation field very broadly—I don't focus on one aspect, such as personal injury or medical malpractice. I personally find that limiting in terms of my own interest and growth. I ask myself, Who would find great value in getting help with their issues? Where would a neutral third party bring value? Then I talk to those people. Consequently, I not only do personal injury and contract disputes but also work with family businesses, partnerships, dysfunctional teams, joint ventures, union-management, and others. This opens up the market quite a bit.

Gary Furlong

community with trade associations and journals. You can also affiliate with people who don't use mediators but who refer cases to lawyers. "We write articles and do a lot of public speaking, from brown bag luncheons to CLE programs," says Dallas mediator Jeff Abrams. "And, although I do not litigate anymore, I believe it's important to be a familiar face around the courthouse so that judges and lawyers know me and keep me in mind."

You can find many conference and trade association opportunities where the source clients are available. For example, associations of corporate council members refer cases to large law firms to handle. If members of these associations know and trust you, they will influence their attorneys who are litigating the cases in selecting a mediator. I've had many cases referred to me by lawyers I didn't know personally but who told me their general counsel recommended me.

If you're interested in class action cases, once or twice a year all the attorneys who do these huge cases meet in Las Vegas and spend two days talking about class action and mass torts. For $200 or $300 you can attend these conferences and meet the people who do these huge cases. I wish I had the time to attend all of these myself!

There are many such opportunities out there: claims adjusters associations, such as RIMS (Risk and Insurance Management Society); risk managers associations; human resources professionals associations, such as PIHRA (Professionals in Human Resources Association)—all of these are very influential in referring matters to outside lawyers who handle employment cases. You can't join everything, but you can test the waters, and you can easily book speaking engagements at these organizations. Identify your niche, then spend some time in research and talking to people to identify the two or three associations that work with lawyers so that you can get them interested in you before they even go to their lawyers. They are the source.

Make a Phone Call, Send a Note

It's a truism that the last person you spoke to is the first person on your mind. So simply making direct calls to clients, former clients, and people you want for clients is a great way to remind them that you're there.

"At one point," says Rick Weiler, "I had what I called 'the last-minute mediation club.' I'd send an email out to every lawyer on the list, informing them of empty dates on my calendar for mediations in the next two weeks. This kept my name in front of them—and we always got new cases." Of course, your approach doesn't have to be this formal. A simple call to say, "Hi, how's it going?" can be enough.

And always remember your database. "Keep track of the lawyers you mediate with," says Weiler. "You build a practice by staying in touch with them. Of the two thousand lawyers in my database, I see some every month, some once a year. There is no more valuable business asset than your contact database."

A Good Marketing Curve

I have a limited time to market, and I don't hire someone to market for me. I mine my previous clients because they're so much more receptive than people I haven't worked with before. I keep track of the cases I've mediated for each client. I write down the dates and what happened. If I get in touch with them later, I can refer to the case as a point of contact. If I get a mediation that does well, I can often track bookings from that client in thirty days. That's a good marketing curve!

Rick Russell

"Name recognition and reputation is the key, and along with that goes communication," says Jeff Abrams. "We send out cards to our database on a regular basis, and we try to demonstrate our creativity in what we send out. Our clients have come to expect our cards, and often they keep them on display in their offices. We like to make people smile, and hope that when they see the cards and smile, they think of us."

"Sometimes I do what I call 'shaking the tree,'" says Toronto's Rick Russell. "If I see that my book of business is sort of thin, I just go into my contact list and start calling people to say, 'Hi, how are you doing? You're a good client, I haven't seen you for a while, what's up?' And while we're talking, I can look at my database, see what kind of work we've done together, refer to an old case to ask how it's coming along, and ask if there's some way we might be able to help them. It's rather transparent, but people seem to like it. It doesn't always turn around work immediately, but it often pays off within a month or two. The thing you've done is brought yourself to mind. If they haven't mediated with you for six months, you might as well not exist."

BOOK SPEAKING ENGAGEMENTS

Susan Hammer is a great proponent of speaking as a way to get visibility. "Every group is looking for speakers," she says. "Never pass up an opportunity to speak." It's true—if you look for opportunities to speak, you will find them. But remember to do your homework first. Make the most of speaking opportunities by knowing the audience you are courting and preparing yourself as a speaker.

Know Your Audience

I learned the hard way how important it is to target a speech to an audience. Many years ago, the Association of Intellectual Property Lawyers asked me to speak at their seminar, and I accepted. I gave a really good speech on mediation. But afterward, their response was lukewarm—at best. When I ran into some of these lawyers at other events, they didn't even remember me. When I finally figured out what went wrong, it seemed obvious: I'd given a speech on mediation, which is what they asked me to do—but I never once related it to intellectual property.

We naturally connect with people who share our worldview and speak our language. Belatedly, I understood that if I had been one of them—if I had been interested in intellectual property law, if I had attended their functions in the past and said, "Oh, by the way, I'm mediating intellectual property cases"—I would have addressed my speech to their issues automatically. And they would have listened and remembered me. But more important, I would have been able to feel their pain. What are the things that really cause them serious concern when confronted with an intellectual property dispute? And with that comprehensive understanding I would have

Giving Value

My only basic rules for speaking are that the talks are an hour or less, and I give them an overview with some specifics and invite them to talk to me directly if they have other questions or situations they'd like to discuss privately. I offer value, though, by teaching them a few basic models or frameworks through which to begin to understand conflict—it's not a sales pitch for an hour. Because I always give more value than I ask, clients are always motivated to work with me again.

Gary Furlong

naturally focused my speech on the things that make them lose sleep at night, letting them know that there is somebody out there who can help.

But in this case, I failed because I wasn't on the inside. Their impression of me was, "Yeah, he gave a decent speech . . . but what was his name again?" There was nothing authentic about me for them. Showing up wasn't enough. I had wasted a great opportunity.

"I was lucky," says Eric Galton. "I was one of the first guys, but I also knew I wouldn't be alone for long. I spoke at thirty-five state bar CLE programs in my first two years of practice—anything to get in front of lawyers. My goal was to create a statewide and even national practice, not just an Austin practice. I did charitable projects, some highly visible pro bono, and many lectures in law firms about representing clients at mediation. Speeches in front of mediator groups are résumé builders and fun events to meet colleagues, but they don't get you work."

Controlling the Room

In any speaking situation—just as at the negotiation table—you want to make sure you control the room. First, make sure they ask *you*, not you and a bunch of other people, to talk to the group. Lawyers in particular have a lot of lunches they have to attend to get credits. If you're the only speaker, all eyes are naturally on you. (For this reason, I don't advise mediators to take part in general panel discussions, because nobody hires talking heads. Panels are just not set up in your interest—you're basically giving away your valuable information and not getting much back in return.)

Once they're looking at you, make sure you hold on to them by making your presentation interactive. Engage and connect with the people in the room and let them see who you are. Find out what their concerns are when dealing with conflict, then address them in your talk. This is probably the most powerful thing you can do.

With almost any kind of group, I never launch directly into my speech. Instead, I let the audience initiate the topic. I say, "Before we start I'd like to go around the room and identify the issues you want to talk about, what your interests are, what you hope to learn today." Then we spend some time writing these questions and issues on a whiteboard. Now, here's the best part: I already know that what I'm going to talk about will address their concerns, because I've done some homework on who they are, and I know my topic. There are generally few surprises. But engaging the audience members in this way makes them feel heard before we even start, creates a mutual connection, and allows me to focus even more.

If this sounds familiar, it should. The overall principle is the same as in mediation: you let the parties speak, you listen to discover their needs and desired outcomes, and you deliver that. And always remember Susan Hammer's cogent warning: "Use Power-Point sparingly! Don't read text to your audience!"

GET INVOLVED IN
MEDIATION ORGANIZATIONS

"If you're doing well," says Rick Weiler, "it creates an obligation to put something back in. So I'm fairly active in the major ADR organizations. That kind of thing has allowed me to see how other mediators are doing, to have some input."

All of the successful mediators who contributed to this book have powerhouse résumés when it comes to serving in mediation organizations. Many have been on the board of directors or served as president; chaired committees; authored books, treatises, and articles; taught workshops to judges and lawyers; and generally been totally focused on career development and mentoring others. And they're willing to give their time on a volunteer basis to help expand their profession, because they have a passion for it. I can earn more money in one day mediating than I do in a semester teaching, but I teach because I still get excited about it.

Of course, there's a danger in getting too involved. It can be an excuse for not putting more time into your business in other ways, and it can also create a type of clutter if you become overly involved and distracted with organizations that probably will not get you business. It's important to give back to your community and your colleagues, but don't become involved simply because you've got nothing else to do.

Be deliberate with your time. Be absolutely certain you like the people you're going to hang out with. If it becomes too political or too competitive or just too aggravating for you to attend, it's obviously not meant to be. A few years ago I was president of a couple of organizations, but I eventually discovered that this was not the best role for me. I like people, but I'm not good at running meetings. I like to act, not react. If I can serve as a resource or adviser, I'm happy to do it. I'm willing to contribute if it expands the field and makes it better for all of us. Every person quoted in this book

Creating a Client Resource

When I started, there were no other private mediators in my area. I wanted to create a resource list for my clients, and I also wanted to generate referrals for my services. I went through the phone book and other resources, and came up with fifty or sixty lawyers, children's therapists, accountants, doctors—people who help people in divorce. I decided not to select randomly, but to find top people in the community. I called and said, "I do divorce mediation. I would like to meet with you to find out what you do because I want you to be a resource for my clients—someone who is an additional option to help them as they go through their divorce." I picked only people whom I really was interested in using as a resource. There had to be integrity in my statement that I would put them on the referral list, because otherwise it wouldn't be genuine.

I quickly learned that if I said to people, "I'd like to take you out to lunch to find out about you so that I can send you business," and spent about forty-five minutes hearing about them, then I could say, "To get on my list you'll need to understand how I work, so let me explain what I do." So I would spend the next fifteen minutes explaining the process, hand them a brochure, and say, "Keep me in mind."

Nina Meierding

contributes to the field voluntarily, but most no longer have the time or inclination to head an organization.

What organizations are you involved in? Who is the audience? The local mediation groups really preach to the local up-and-coming mediators. That's fine for a short time. But if you intend to be very successful, you'll find that you don't have time to spend with that type of organization. Your target audience is the gatekeepers of the cases you're interested in, and that's where you need to put your time and energy.

CREATE A USER-FRIENDLY WEB SITE

Let me just put it right out there: with a few exceptions, such as Jeff and Hesha Abrams's card campaign, paper is a waste of time and money. If you're thinking of putting money into brochures, stop. In today's wired world, an Internet presence is a must. Ralph Williams states the situation baldly: "Half the organized bar is under the age of thirty-five. They expect you to have a Web site, to have email, and to be able to open their attached brief with any of three programs. If I didn't have a Web site, I would be considered a Luddite, which would impact my credibility. The Web site is assumed—it's not something that distinguishes you. You've got to have it because it's part of the package people expect."

"Our Web site has been very good for us," says Rick Russell. "In our area of work, people do shop for professionals this way. It's a good way to get the first phone call, and it's also for closing the deal from the phone call."

Today, when people want to learn more about you, they go to the Web. And if they don't see what they want there, they'll probably go elsewhere. "I'll do anything to get people to go to my Web site," says Jeff Kichaven. "That's how people shop these days. One lawyer will say to another lawyer, 'I like these three mediators.' The first thing the second lawyer will do is go to our Web sites and check us out. So having a professional, first-rate Web site is essential today, just as it is in every other business."

On another side of the world, New Zealand mediator Geoff Sharp agrees. "Having a Web site is invaluable at a local level—it is an efficient way of directing people to terms of engagement, standard mediation agreement, bio, and so on. Many of my phone calls are inquiries and, even in the middle of a mediation, I am able to direct people to the Web site and have them check me out while I am working rather than my having to send them material once I am back at my computer."

Essentially, I want my Web site to give potential clients the easy way to get information about me, fast. So my Web site is my biography, my business card, and more. Yet it's not designed as a destination site. Why? Because there's a lot of information available on the Internet that's a lot better than I could ever put up, and it's constantly being updated by others. If you create a site that needs constant updating, you're metaphorically cluttering your desk. I have a lot of good information and articles on my site, but it's mostly archived.

When people are thinking of me as a mediator, they want to know the basics—who I am, what I've done, my scheduling and fees—and that's the first thing they see. If they want to learn more about me, they can see my recent cases and where I've been published, and even read articles I've written. If they want to learn more about mediation, they can link to valuable resources.

You want to create a Web site that's creative, simple to navigate, and easy to access and that includes basic information about you: your background, how to contact you, your policies, and a library of your articles or media clips. Personally, I would rather have people see my picture quickly, see that some great things have been written about me, and then call me. If they want to check me out later, they can go back and read the articles. Your site doesn't have to be expensive, but it has to reflect your character and be so simple to navigate that it doesn't turn people away.

The Path of Least Resistance

If your boss says, "Find me five potential mediators," it's human nature to use the path of least resistance: go to the Web. If you find ten potential mediators, and five of them have information you can download and print, you're going to print those five. You're not going to go to the one-page Web site that just says, "Call me" and call that person. My philosophy on marketing is to make it easier for the potential user.

Mediators who don't use the Internet for marketing are missing the competitive advantage. This is not the future; it's the present.

Robert A. Creo

The point of my Web site is to give people a teaser that compels them to call me. Too much information causes overload and prevents people from being curious. If they think they know enough about me already, why would they call me? I'm looking to make an initial connection through my Web site that will lead to a more personal connection.

By contrast, many mediators have much more on their Web sites, and they find it works well for them. Robert A. Creo, who gets great value from his Web site, says, "The easier you can make it for them, by having more information, the better." Personally, I just found it was too much work to keep up an information-rich site! If you're Internet friendly and willing to invest the time, however, your Web site can be valuable marketing tool.

Creo is a big proponent of using the Internet for marketing. "I have a very active Web site and I have a lot of information on it,"

Point of Sale

We invested a lot of money in our Web site years earlier than our competition did. Before that, we used to send out an awful lot of information kits. They cost us at least $10 each to send out. Well, the Web site has all that information—and people can print it out, using their own paper, while they're talking to you. If they come off a conversation with you and feel good about you, and they can go on your Web site immediately to learn more, there's no holding you back. That's point of sale!

Rick Russell

he says. "I think Web sites are a good source of information, and getting that information is not intrusive. If you're shopping for mediators, you may be reluctant to call and engage the mediator in a dialogue because you think the mediator may put the sell on you. This way, you can go to the Web site, download the information, and no one knows you were there. This is more beneficial to the mediator than never receiving a call in the first place.

"Also," he points out, "the lawyers making the decision about the mediator are usually not the people calling the mediator. They delegate that to their secretaries or associates, and the younger those people are, the more likely they are to use the Internet. They'd rather email somebody than pick up the phone and call. They're used to receiving information through the medium of screen, and they're much more comfortable doing their investigation on the Internet than the old-fashioned way, by phone."

Jeff Abrams says, "I refer people to our Web site all the time for more information about us. I also ask for testimonials from lawyers and parties. If they had a very positive experience in a training or mediation, I ask if they wouldn't mind writing a letter to that effect and allowing us to put an excerpt on our Web site. This is a good way of continuing to build a strong reputation."

Will your Web site get you more business? A lot of mediators, including some at the top of the field, pour time and energy into their sites, convinced that an innovative Internet presence brings business. I can't prove it doesn't, but I believe that these mediators are at the top not because of their Web sites but because of their reputation and referrals and the story people are telling about them. Your Web site will give you some credibility, but don't become so involved in creating and updating it that you forget your main marketing task: getting out there and working the room!

USE EMAIL WISELY

For those of us who began our careers fifteen or more years ago and remember email with big green letters glowing against a black background, it's important not to underestimate the speed and importance of email today. We use it to check schedules, keep in touch with colleagues, follow up on cases, and thank parties at the end of a case. As you probably already know, it's important to harvest email addresses from clients and potential clients so that you can use them in the future for email newsletters, thank-yous, and other contacts.

Answering email even has to be figured in as a part of your workday. "It's very clear that the top people in the field are doing their emails at the beginning and end of the day," says Robert A. Creo. "You don't just sit by your machine and, when an email comes in, answer it."

Avoid the Crackberry Syndrome

Most mediators these days carry a BlackBerry or Treo to get their email during the day. It's important to respond to email in a timely manner, but avoid what I call the Crackberry syndrome—becoming so obsessed with your portable technology that you ignore the people you're with.

I view mediation as a profession. Is your physician checking his BlackBerry in the middle of an exam? No way! You're not present with your clients if you're constantly checking your email or getting vibrated by your PDA or cell phone. My rule is, never have your cell phone on when you're working or meeting with clients or potential clients. Wait until you're alone to check your email, and take that bluetooth device out of your ear. Be fully present.

Email Newsletters

Email newsletters have effectively replaced their paper predecessors, although anti-spam legislation limits the ability to send mass mailings easily. Even computerphobic mediators are beginning to use email more and more, and in creative ways. "If someone has a good experience at a mediation and I follow up in a few days with a thank-you by email, I always make sure to attach my résumé," says Rick Russell. "I ask them to keep it on hand and forward it to anyone of their acquaintance who may be in need of mediation. All they need to do is click Forward. I can get so much done with so little effort."

People get a lot of spam. Just sending out newsletters to get your name in front of them may have a boomerang effect. Make sure your newsletter provides tremendous value and is not just something that will be viewed as gratuitous marketing. And make sure your newsletter is received on an opt-in basis: ask permission to put people's names on your mailing list *before* you send them your latest gem.

A number of successful mediators send email newsletters regularly to the names on their database. "I record every new person I meet in my leather journal and include details about where I met them, and when, and—most important—what their interests are," says Michelle Obradovic. "I ask them if they have any kind of newsletter or mailing list that I could get on, and I always ask if they would mind if I add them to my email list. I always add them into

The Daily Quotation Email

The significant problems we face cannot be solved by the same level of thinking that created them.
— Albert Einstein

What can you do proactively in terms of email without making yourself a pest? When I send any email, at the bottom of the email I have little box that has what I call my "Daily Quotation"—a famous quote and a few personal comments. It changes every day, seven days a week. And at the bottom it refers the reader to read the Daily Quotations I have archived on my Web site.

Robert A. Creo

---

my database before the next edition of my newsletter. Sometimes I send a follow-up note with a tidbit of information that might be helpful to their business.

"I publish a newsletter every month," she explains. "I take a day when I'm not mediating and write four at a time. Then I send it to my personal contact database—about five thousand names every month. Adjusters, business people, accountants—anyone I've come in contact with. So I write it for a general audience. Every month I get responses back. I average about fifteen cases for every newsletter I send out."

Rick Russell is enthusiastic about the ease of creating electronic newsletters. "You can create one newsletter and, by cutting and pasting, create two or three different versions—we'll send one to commercial mediation clients, one to workplace mediation clients,

Use a Variety of Approaches

Everyone has a different learning style—visual, auditory, kinesthetic—and I think it's important to use different approaches. We send cards and written materials because it can be important to have something tactile in your hands. If people are more visual, they can go to our Web site, read our CVs, and see our photos. And thank-you phone calls are always welcome.

Jeff Abrams

one to corporate mediation clients, and one to our facilitation clients. You get a lot of leverage out of the time you put into it."

Ralph Williams has been very successful with his email newsletter, which always includes a brief ADR tip. "The people on my list are people who are either in the mediation business or close to it, or they are my customers," he says. The newsletter runs a couple of hundred words at the most, and goes out once a month to about twenty-two hundred people. "Every month I get two or three calls and cases that are directly traceable to the newsletter. I can't go to a bar function now and not have at least three people come up to me and say 'I love the tip.' It has to be sent out in batches of twenty-five to miss the spam filters, and I pay my assistant virtually a day's wages just to assemble them and send them out, but I would never let that go. The very last thing I would do is stop writing the monthly ADR tip."

"I don't have a newsletter," says Jeff Kichaven, "but when I have articles published, for example, I'll send a note to the contacts on my email list that it's been published, with a link to the article. You have to send something of value to the person, otherwise email is an imposition—it's a turn-off, not a turn-on."

USE ADVERTISING SPARINGLY

Does it pay to advertise? Sometimes. Sort of.

Advertising in legal or institutional newspapers and magazines serves as a simple reminder that you're still out in the market. Many top mediators still place small ads with their picture for this reason. But if you're going to make that commitment, you'd better be all in—your ad has to run at least a couple of dozen times in the course of a year or year and a half—and don't expect to get business from it.

The more effective marketing vehicle is the personal contact, the writing—things that add value. Nevertheless, for the past ten years I've been running an ad in a trade association journal for trial lawyers. It's my way of letting them know I'm still out there. But, in my opinion, people who invest money in the daily law journals and statewide bar publications are throwing money down the drain. Unless you do it with other people in a group or on a panel, where the expense can be shared with others, the cost is high and the payoff is not great.

Successful mediators have very definite opinions about advertising. "I find that it is a waste of money to do generic mass-market ads," says Michelle Obradovic. "Mediation is a personal service, and it requires a personal touch. All of my marketing materials reflect my personality."

"We do some advertising in the law report service in Ontario every three weeks," says Rick Russell. "It's just a third of a page with our pictures—for name recognition. It's to make people say, 'Oh, I remember that face; we settled that case.' They have a good association with you, and they think of you. On another level, the ad also says that we're doing well and can afford to be there."

Robert A. Creo emphasizes that if you are going to advertise, frequency trumps size. "In his book *The Evolution of Cooperation*, Robert Axelrod says that frequency of contact enhances cooperation. Not the length, but the frequency. If I'm going to spend an hour with you, and I have sixty minutes of your time, six ten-minute segments are better than one sixty-minute segment for trust and relationship building.

"We're looking for a way to engage frequency of contact," he continues. "A small print ad with the same placement in every issue is better than a half-page ad every so often. You want to focus on frequency of contact, even if it is minimal contact, because over the long run this will build your business and relationships. You have to consider how many impressions of yourself can get out there to the marketplace."

Frequency of contact is very important. Many years ago, when private ads became popular, a small entrepreneurial group of judges created an insert to a legal newspaper. It was a small yellow card with their names and numbers on it, and if you ever needed an arbitrator, you just pulled out this card. Because of its color, it came to be known as the gold card. It was given to the entire legal community, and people would keep it in their drawer. The International Academy of Mediators did a similar thing a few years ago, creating a card with a roster of about twenty neutrals who committed to being on the card for the next five years. When split among so many people, the cost for advertising like that is pretty minimal. And it's the kind of thing people really keep if the quality of mediators is high: frequency of contact and uniqueness are the key.

Finally, a familiar refrain: "Advertise to your target market," advises Cliff Hendler. "Don't use a shotgun approach. Find the vehicle people will go to. In Toronto, the *Ontario Reports* is a weekly journal every lawyer gets—95 percent of our ads go there. In Los Angeles, lawyers read the *Daily Journal*. Is your market lawyers? Businesspeople? Family people? Target to your specialty."

WRITING GIVES YOU CREDIBILITY

Writing, if it's something you enjoy, is another way to get your name in front of people. Your name in print—particularly if you have something interesting and innovative to say—gives you credibility and visibility. Remember, the market has gotten fairly mature and educated, so writing an article about basic mediation theory could put you in the wrong light. Be careful not to regurgitate what's already been written. People are looking for creative thinkers, writers who will push the technology of mediation theory so that the readers are able to learn new things. Try to be inspirational. Don't just demonstrate the value of the process. Offer different strategies others can integrate into their practices.

Be sure to archive your articles on your Web site. This demonstrates to clients and potential clients that you have published, and gives them the opportunity to read the articles if they wish. "I write articles for a variety of publications read by people who use our services," says Rick Russell. "My partner, Gary Furlong, has written two books. You can publish chapters of your books on your Web site, and people can go on your site and print off a chapter. It gives you a certain amount of credibility with people if you have a book you can put on a Web site."

Nearly all the contributors to this book write fairly regularly, and there is no shortage of places to publish, including *Conflict Resolution Quarterly*, *Dispute Resolution* magazine, *Alternatives*, and many others. "Every bar association has a publication," says Ralph Williams. "It is surprisingly easy to find places to publish. And if you're going to write, keep writing."

The question is, who is your audience? Why write for a national trade publication if your real clients come from your local geographical region? In terms of measurable impact on your calendar, an article in a small section of one of your local bar newsletters will probably bring more clients than an article in the American Bar Association journal.

TEACHING AS A MARKETING STRATEGY

I fell into teaching in the early 1990s when I participated in a workshop on mediation given to a group of judges. Randy Lowry, the director of the Straus Institute for Dispute Resolution at Pepperdine University, was also involved in the workshop. We hit it off right away, and he invited me to breakfast the next day, at which time he asked me to teach a mediation course and be director of dispute resolution. I said, "But I've never taught before." Fortunately, that didn't deter him. I then observed Randy and Peter Robinson present the Mediating the Litigated Case program. They were dramatic and well organized, and really knew how to connect with their students. I studied their approaches diligently and became director of the Mediating the Litigated Case program.

When it comes to teaching, you don't do it for the money; you do it for the fun of it and to support your credibility and visibility. In terms of all these factors, being connected with a school like Pepperdine is about as good as it gets. It promotes its programs heavily—four-color brochures with biographies and ads. So at what was essentially the beginning of my career, every time the school offered the six-day course, it sent a beautiful brochure with my biography to almost every lawyer in California. And this was at no expense to me—Pepperdine paid for the privilege. That brochure gave me a lot of instant credibility, which helped because I didn't come from a judicial background.

One of the benefits of teaching lawyers about mediation is that they become great referral sources. Most of them soon find that despite their good intentions, they are not able to develop a practice because they want to keep their day jobs. But through the Pepperdine workshops they become intrigued with the process and find that they want to mediate their cases. When they're looking for a mediator, the first person they think of is the director of the course!

Teaching also improved my public speaking capabilities. Public speaking can be scary, and most people aren't comfortable with it.

Don't Dismiss Teaching

I teach several university courses. Originally, it didn't give rise to a lot of mediation work, and I was a bit puzzled. But now it's making more of a difference. It turns out that people who take the courses refer people who have disputes to their teachers. Students can't ethically take on a friend's case, but they believe in the process and want to pass the person on to someone they have confidence in. That's happily been a growth area for me. I almost dismissed it as a marketing strategy, but I wouldn't dismiss it now.

Rick Russell

If they do it, they do it in such a bland way that they turn people off. After some years of teaching, I learned what it takes to be engaging and entertaining. In fact, teaching turned out to be a personal growth opportunity because I improved my skills, met people, and got many more requests for speaking. Teaching opens doors.

On the downside, teaching is not a profit center. You can be extremely busy and popular while your business is actually foundering. Some people decide to become mediation trainers because their actual practices are not generating enough business to support them. Eventually they get so involved in serving as workshop leaders that they forget their goal of practicing mediation for a living. Be cautious about getting caught up in that.

One last point: don't feel you have to teach if you're not drawn to it. Remember that high school history teacher who looked like he'd rather be anywhere else than in the classroom? An unengaged teacher doesn't accomplish much real teaching. Not every top mediator enjoys teaching or is willing to make the sacrifices it entails. Some are quite comfortable drawing their boundaries. Joe Epstein says simply, "I'm not willing to give up my evenings to teach."

GET BUSY!

"The number of hours I spend marketing far outstrips the number of hours I spend mediating," says Jeff Kichaven. "It's a very competitive field." When you're the product *and* the marketer, marketing becomes a natural and inevitable part of what you do.

"I treat client development the way some people treat running for public office," says Michelle Obradovic. "I am always prepared to make a quick toast or pose for a picture or tell a joke. I write a monthly column and send it to all of my personal contacts, about five thousand, by email. I also teach a mediation advocacy class for third-year students at the local law school, and I guest lecture on negotiation skills to the entire first-year class during their first semester. I also guest lecture at an evening unaccredited law school each semester and at another local university for the justice science majors. A bar association luncheon or a CLE program is also something that I usually do once a month."

Think about providing CLE programs for free—one-hour lunch programs at law firms. The lawyers get credits for attending, and you get exposure. If I were just starting, I would do more of these.

The more types of marketing you do, the more important it becomes to stay organized. Create a schedule of projects you are working on, and set timeline goals for completion. And remember to check them off when they're done!

"Success," says Robert Jenks, "is a function of personal investment on your part: focus your energy. I know a guy who was just starting out as a mediator. He wrote to five hundred people he knew or had interacted with in his personal career to tell them he had

Never Rest!

I thought having a mediation practice would be like having an insurance brokerage: you get the pipeline full, and it goes on cruise control. But as a mediator you have to keep hustling all the time—changing what you do, distinguishing yourself from what others are doing. The mediation training programs are grinding out new mediators as fast as law schools grind out lawyers. I'm working as hard to keep "top of mind" now as I was in the beginning. The last person they talk to is the first person they think of.

Never rest!

Michael Landrum

started a business, then he called or visited as many of them as he could. His practice took off like a rocket because he was focused. He invested the energy, and out of that he reaped something."

"You have to do a lot of business development," says Robert A. Creo. "You find time for all this stuff because you can work anywhere now, with BlackBerries and cell phones and laptops.

"I'm a Type A, task oriented," he says. "I like to check off what's done. I can't waste time. Lawyers are time conscious, used to breaking things into tenth of an hour segments. When you don't want to waste even one six-minute segment, it becomes almost a compulsion. You've got to love it or you're not going to be happy."

A final reminder: when you're out there getting busy, talking to people, teaching courses, working hard, you have to remember the basic paradox: even though you're doing all this in the furtherance of your understanding and your career, if you want to build a sub-

The Exception That Proves the Rule

When you work on your own, the only pressure is what you put on yourself. I'm quite happy. Last year was a record year for revenue for me in this business. I wanted more free time, so I said to my wife, "Let's dial it back a little bit. We'll earn less but have a little more free time." So we did, and we did have more free time—but, due to fee increases, we're actually ahead financially!

Rick Weiler

---

stantial practice, *it can never be about you*. You have to go out there—whether it's a cocktail party or a training course—ready to listen to other people and discover what they want. You're not out there to tell people how great you are, but to find out what's going on in their practice and how you can help. When they remember your name and face, that's the subliminal message they should receive on their radar screen.

TOP-TIER STRATEGIES

1. **Work the butterfly effect to your advantage.**

    The effect of your relatively small marketing efforts—a training, a speaking engagement, or even a brief conversation with the person sitting next to you on a plane—can often result in surprisingly big gains. The secret is the invisible connections. You can't hope to control or even know about all the connections, but you can have faith that the more you get out there, the more people will know about you and your work. Putting yourself in opportunity's way means that running into the right people at the right time is really more than luck: eventually, people who need your help and cases you were born to mediate can't help but bump right into you.

2. **Decide who your clients will be and then put yourself where they can see you.**

   This is a fairly simple formula. Study the pool of potential clients. Look for well-established, cohesive business communities with trade associations and journals. You can also affiliate with people who don't use mediators but who refer cases to lawyers. Once you've targeted your client pool, attend their conferences and meetings of their trade associations or specialized attorney groups, and start making acquaintances. You'll learn essential information, make important contacts, and impress people with the effort you put into your work. Remember to collect names, vital information, and email addresses for your ever-expanding database.

3. **Check in periodically with the people in your client database.**

   It's true that the last person we speak to is usually the first person who comes to mind. When people are looking for a mediator, you want to be that person. Make effective use of your downtime by calling to check in with clients and potential clients. See what's on their plate and ask if there's any way you can help ease their load.

4. **Book speaking engagements to your target groups.**

   There's no shortage of opportunities to book speaking engagements, but it's important to ensure that you're speaking to a group that will actually generate clients for you. Target your talk to the group and do everything you can to answer their questions and respond to their needs.

5. Be an interesting and interactive speaker.

Follow these five basic rules for speaking, and you will reap not only return engagements but new clients eager to use your expertise: (1) make sure that you are the sole speaker; (2) control the room; (3) discover your audience's problems and give them solutions; (4) make sure your presentation is interactive; (5) speak to your audience's worldview and use their language.

6. Use the Internet to your advantage.

Everybody needs a Web site, but it's not necessary to go overboard. The main point is to get potential clients to make personal contact. Make sure your site gives them your basic biography and stats, articles you have published, and complimentary words that have been written about you, but not so much that they feel overloaded with information. Design it to be easy to navigate. If you have the time, energy, and inclination to create an email newsletter, regular mailings can be an effective way to keep your name in the front of people's minds. Just be sure to offer interesting and new information. Do all you can to make sure your newsletter isn't identified as spam!

7. Advertise judiciously.

Use advertising as another way to keep your name and face in people's minds, but don't use it in such a way that it cheapens your image or commodifies you. Frequency and good taste trump size every time.

8. If you have the talent and enjoy the process, write articles.

Your name in print is a quick route to credibility and visibility. It is crucial, however, to write about something new, put an intriguing spin on something that's been around for a while, or describe a technique people can use in their own practice. It's also crucial to publish where other mediators, and your target audience, are most likely to be—it's not worth your while to write for a large general readership.

9. Make teaching a marketing strategy.

Teaching or leading trainings can be a wonderful way to share your gift, and an interesting way to find new clients. Students—most of whom are lawyers—frequently think of their instructors when they need a mediator. Be sure, however, that you don't devote so much time to teaching that you neglect your practice.

10. Take your marketing seriously.

Marketing—getting out there, meeting people, and being seen and heard—is almost another full-time job, but it's indispensable if your goal is to make it to the top tier of mediators. Get busy, work hard, and have fun doing it.

5

Practical Considerations
The Business of Mediation

*If you can't make a living, you can't provide the
service. So it's important that you know how to make
a living!*

Chris Moore

Highly successful mediators have to be good entrepreneurs. Just mediating well will not keep you in business.

"Well-developed mediation skills and an impressive list of mediated cases do not yield a sustainable mediation practice," agrees one successful mediator. "It takes knowing good business practices; having the discipline to follow them; confidence; balance; and the ability to innovate, to lead, and to inspire others. You have to be excellent at all of it: good service, good businessperson—you have to do it all." And, I would add, you may have to be willing to try out different business models until you find the right fit.

Mediators pride themselves on being creative thinkers, so it's no surprise that there is no one-size-fits-all business model for mediators. Each of the top-tier mediators whose voices fill this book has a unique practice developed over time and tailored to fit his or her needs, interests, preferences, and personality. Here's a small sample that typifies their wide range of styles:

"I've had partnerships and been on panels," says Robert A. Creo. "Now I work by myself."

"I have two partners, and we run a panel of fifty-some mediators," says Robert Jenks.

"I've never liked the sole practitioner model," says Gary Furlong. "I own a small company with a partner, Rick Russell, and a few associates. I find that the critical mass of having four or five colleagues putting the company name out there helps a great deal."

"I'm in a suite I share with lawyers who are not mediators," says Paul Monicatti. "I've been with some of them almost twenty-five years. We run our own separate practices."

"I've been a partner for twenty-five years with CDR Associates in Boulder, Colorado, a nonprofit conflict resolution agency," says Bernie Mayer. "Four partners organized and started the place. Now we're trying to turn it over to the next generation of people."

"I started mediating in 1990 as a sole practitioner," says Cliff Hendler. "But if you get sick or want to go on vacation, and it's just you. . . . I also decided to create a firm because I wanted to have something to sell or pass on to my kids when I retired, and I'm a gregarious type—I like to work in a crowd of people."

"Our business model is two partners, with an associate who pays a royalty," says another successful mediator. "She shares our office space, and I refer a fair amount of work to her. Her royalty covers part of the overhead and contributes toward the profit. Another associate pays a royalty—his share coming back for the fact that we're the place that got called. And when he refers cases to me, I pay him a referral fee."

The quick lesson is, there's no one perfect business model, and there's no certain path to success. Robert Jenks jokes about his firm, MAPS, the largest mediation and arbitration firm in the Southern United States. "There's one thing that sets us apart," he explains with a smile. "If there's a mistake to be made, we've made it! That's our claim to fame. There's no cookie cutter for this business. If there's a blind alley we've been down it. It's a process. You learn from your mistakes as well as from your successes. We've built our business on our mistakes!"

If you're searching for the business model that fits you, look to yourself, your interests, your unique personality, and your past achievements. If you once worked with a big law firm and enjoyed the structure, you might eventually fit in well as part of a large provider group that takes care of your billings and marketing. If you were good at getting business in an earlier career, the same will hold true for you as a mediator. If you're the gregarious type, a partnership or collaboration might be your choice. And if you're anything like me, you'll fly solo and find your own way.

EVOLUTION OF A PRACTICE

Most successful mediators stay that way by evolving their practice over time in response to the market and to their own interests. "We hit it at the upside of the curve," says Bernie Mayer, speaking of the evolution of CDR. "We were very innovative, applying new concepts to areas that were ready to go. Diversification was helpful then, but now the field calls for specialization, so we developed that as well. We were very good at applying what we knew to new areas, we did good work, and the combination of training and mediation was a good one for us."

Like that of most of the mediators who have shared their thoughts for this book, my practice has evolved over time—and it's still evolving.

By the early 1990s, my business was growing along with the field in general. As one of the first attorney mediators in Los Angeles, I took on whatever I could get—fender benders, insurance, real estate. I tried different business models. I started out as a provider and formed First Mediation Corporation—I was the main mediator, but

I would also recruit others to be on the panel. After a while, however, I realized that I didn't want to be a promoter for other people. It was profitable, but it wasn't my calling.

So I reconfigured my business model as just me: Jeff Krivis, private mediator. My thinking went like this: when you need heart surgery, your first choice isn't to walk into the hospital and take whoever's on duty. You call the best heart surgeon in town. I figured that lawyers and businesses that were looking for mediators would naturally come to someone they'd heard of and liked. In my experience—though this is certainly not true for everyone—a mediator who works for a provider risks becoming a dispensable commodity. So I shifted my model and promoted myself.

Now, clients who seek me out are specifically seeking *my* services rather than any one of several people on a roster. I still have First Mediation, but I use it as an entity to do billing and to run my pension account, and because some companies will hire only "vendors."

MENTORING

Successful mediators are, by definition, busy all the time. Our business tends to be so absorbing that we need some time to clear out our minds. Sooner or later, the need for free time becomes important for personal health and sanity. After many years of working at full speed, I recently made a decision that working five and six long days a week, every week, is no longer appealing. So, for the first time, I've taken on an associate, Mariam Zadeh, to help with overflow. We work together as mentor and apprentice, and we both profit from the relationship.

Market Segmentation

I have come to see this arrangement as akin to the concept of segmentation in the marketplace. At Bath & Body Works, for example, the CEO broke the chain into three tiers: flagship stores, middle-tier stores, and top of the line stores. According to the CEO, market segmentation unlocks growth potential by creating competition and opportunities at various levels within the organization. In a similar way, you might say that I have segmented my market with Mariam. Because she is just starting her career as a mediator, we are telling our market—that is, lawyers—that she is available for cases I might not handle, such as smaller damage cases. Clients appreciate it because they get someone who was trained by me and has learned my closing techniques but charges less. My firm gets to keep business it normally wouldn't retain because I might have priced myself out of the market or simply had no openings in my calendar. And Mariam appreciates it because she is getting referrals, earning money, and making contact with potential new clients.

There are less formal ways of mentoring, of course. Jeff Abrams says, "I have informally mentored a number of new mediators, and I see great potential in their ability and skills. They are interested, excited, and committed to the work of mediation. During her first few mediations, for example, one woman would call me between caucuses to brainstorm what to do next. She and I have established a good relationship over time and distance, and she is a very successful mediator today. It's a great process with people who are interested and where there's a right fit. There's no financial remuneration involved; I just want to see them succeed."

Observation can be an excellent teaching medium, especially if the mentor takes the time to direct the observers. "I have a lot of people come watch me mediate," says Cliff Hendler. "I'm selective, because I want them to be people who are committed to the field. They're fascinated by the process, and I try hard to have them put their focus on the process rather than the issues. I tell them that they're there to watch the dynamics and figure out what's going on, where they might see the source of conflict and of opportunity. I don't want them to come up to me afterward and tell me who was right and who was wrong. I want them to tell me the mood of the room, who was listening to whom."

The Benefits of Mentoring

I have gotten much more out of mentoring than simply hiring someone to take cases. My role as mentor has actually helped expand my perspective on the practice of mediation, and I believe it is helping me become better at what I do. I spent many years doing little more than waking up, doing a case, coming home, preparing for the next case . . . and waking up the next morning and doing it again. I enjoyed it, but I have to admit: that was pretty narrow! Now I have the opportunity to think about what somebody else is working on, discuss case strategies with her, and help her expand her own book of business. Being a mentor allows me to reach out beyond the boundaries I created over the last ten years or so and help shape the future.

I have also found being a mentor to be inspirational. I no longer have the same kind of ambition to go out and do all the things we mention in this book. But the person I am mentoring is younger, highly motivated, at the beginning of her career, and very interested in learning and doing all of it. This kind of energy is contagious!

Today, mediation is highly competitive. We're inundated with new mediators who take a forty-hour training and think they can mediate. As Jeff Kichaven puts it, "All you need is a business card that says 'Mediator' and you're a mediator." As successful professionals, we need to look beyond competition to the future of our profession. Right now, the mediation field is heavy on the experienced end. Where's that knowledge going to go if we're not willing to impart it to other people? We don't want to lose that. Older painters and sculptors teach apprentices their art, because they know that if they don't, all their hard-won experience will be lost. The only way to excel and to make sure we train new mediators who are of high quality is to mentor them.

Finding a Mentor Relationship

If you're looking for a mentor, you first have to figure out what your path is, what kind of mediator you want to be, whose style you admire, and who you resonate with. Then get in touch with that person and ask if you can shadow him or her. From there it will either confirm that you want to proceed, or it will be a wake-up call!

When you approach someone to be your mentor, you have to bring something to the relationship. Don't just think about what the mentor can offer you, but how you can add value to your mentor, the person you're seeking value from. It's a two-way street, and you're creating a long-term bond. Any success or defeat you have will reflect on your mentor. You need to be cognizant of that.

I'm a Buddhist, and the mentor-disciple relationship is one of the key elements of the practice. It's all about developing a relationship with someone you respect and having that person guide you, and about your being there for him or her. It's not just about the contacts—"I'm going to introduce you to all these people, and you're going to get a lot of cases." It's about the intricacies of mediating that you don't learn in class or read in a book. That's what people who are starting out need to think about.

If you really want to make your mark in this profession, ask, "Who do I respect in this field? Who do I want to follow?" Don't just go with the most well known person. Find someone you resonate with and then you'll be able to say, "Now I really have a mentor."

Mariam Zadeh

MAKE A PLAN

"A lot of new mediators, especially lawyers, don't have experience with business plans, marketing plans, setting goals," says Jeff Kichaven. "Most people in big law firms are not intimately involved with the business aspect, and they're unprepared to deal with what you need to do to have a successful business as a mediator. Ten years ago, when I left my law firm and went into private practice as a mediator, I said, 'What do I do now?' So I hired a business coach and relied heavily on my CPA, who was very helpful with a lot of business-oriented information."

I cannot overemphasize the importance of having a plan, a way to chart your business goals and keep track of your progress. It can make all the difference between becoming discouraged and leaving the profession and persevering through to success. Nina Meierding

The Straight Story

A lot of people get upset when you give them the straight story: that being an entrepreneur is at least as important as being a good mediator. Sometimes I'll say, "You've got to be prepared to go a substantial period of time without any revenue, and then you've got to be prepared to go a substantial period of time without any income."

They'll say, "Revenue? Income? What's the difference?"

And I'll reply, "Perhaps a mediation practice is not for you."

Jeff Kichaven

puts the problem succinctly: "Many mediators choose the field of conflict resolution because they feel a drive and a commitment to help others resolve their disputes. For some mediators there is almost a missionary zeal in bringing this noble concept to the public's attention. Often this passion means that mediators are not good businessmen or businesswomen. They don't develop business plans, and they idealistically expect to transition from their existing profession to mediation without difficulty."

"What I strive for in my development plan," says Michelle Obradovic, "is to identify the opportunities that I have over the next six months to a year and then to think about how I can structure my business now to make the most of those opportunities in the future. With the operating plan, my goal is to follow it until the value of the prior development plan is captured. These two practices keep me personally grounded and help me gauge the growth of my business."

Goal Tracking

When my associate, Mariam Zadeh, was considering becoming a full-time mediator, I asked her, "How do you know this is what you want to do? Let's think about your goals and what obstacles you might run into." I suggested she put together a goal-tracking sheet, and she ran with it.

"A lot of people say they want to get into mediation," says Zadeh, "but they have no concept of what they want to do. A goal-tracking sheet really helps you sort it out. There are four aspects to creating a goal sheet: (1) setting the goal; (2) exploring the obstacles; (3) brainstorming strategies; and (4) determining the intended result of those efforts. You have to be specific, and you really have to be honest with yourself."

Here is a sample goal tracker you can use at the beginning of your practice or at any point that you want to reframe your goals:

GOAL: *To become a successful mediator*
INTENDED RESULT: *To create a mutually beneficial long-term business relationship with mentor*

Obstacles	Strategies
When to leave current job	• When prerequisites of meeting goal are in place
Maintain mutual trust between self and mentor	• Open communication channels • Honest mutual dealings • Candid expectation setting
Add value to self	• Gain experience and learn from mentor • Discuss fee arrangement with mentor
Add value to mentor	• Expand business and generate additional income • Provide backup during sick/vacation times • More time for speaking engagements
Client management	• Network with existing contacts • Establish new contacts (mentor's overflow and referrals)
Maintain steady cash flow during transition	• Earnings to match current salary • Per diem work
Office space	• To start, coordinate with mentor's schedule; once profitable, expand space

	• Mediate at parties' offices or at outside locations
Managing relationships with mentor's existing employees	• Get tips from mentor on how to create incentives and ease the transition
Work and life balance	• Work hard while making time for personal goals
Downtime during startup phase	• Network
	• Write articles for publication
	• Volunteer on appellate, superior, and federal panels

CAN YOU BE A NEUTRAL IN A LAW FIRM?

As much as we emphasize that success will eventually mean giving up your day job, some highly successful lawyers-turned-mediators do manage to use their law firm as home base for their mediation practice.

"My present business model is not my first choice," says Tracy Allen, "but it is what it is due to other demands, commitments, and necessities unrelated to building a practice. Fortunately, working in a large law firm allows me access to services, facilities, and the 'grapevine' that I wouldn't have in a solo or group ADR practice. That said, however, I know I lose work because I am affiliated with a plaintiff's medical malpractice firm—but I also get work because of the firm's reputation.

"It was easier to begin building the practice from this vantage point," she explains, "as I had other revenue to stay alive. Now I choose how, where, and from whom my revenue is derived, which means I have total autonomy in how hard I want or am willing to work. As long as the money is in the door at year end, my firm

Partnering

In new markets, particularly construction, partnering is a big part of what I do. It's almost like marriage counseling before the marriage, and it's sort of like mediation. You get brought in by one group of people to facilitate, and a lot of people get to see what you do. This gives you an opportunity to develop a relationship with a lot of people.

Rick Russell

---

doesn't care where it comes from. I have a case manager who I can't live without, and she streamlines most of the administrative work and my calendar."

Ben Picker also works as a neutral inside a law firm. "I have had an active practice as a mediator for approximately twenty years," he says. "My story is a bit different from most because I was already well known and well respected as a leader in the legal profession and in the community even before I embarked on my mediation career.

"Initially, my practice as a mediator was part-time only and was combined with an active practice as a litigator in complex commercial disputes and class actions. Over time, it evolved to a full-time practice in ADR and mediation. Since 1995, I have been a partner in Stradley Ronon, a 150-lawyer firm in Philadelphia, and have served as chair of a 10-lawyer ADR practice group.

"I recognize that I am an exception in the world of full-time neutrals, and I would not encourage others to follow my path, for two reasons. First, many assignments cannot be undertaken due to conflicts of interest. Second, many law firms discourage a neutral's practice within a law firm due to the problem of 'downstream conflicts' and the fact that the work cannot be leveraged. At Stradley Ronon, however, I have had the full support of an exceptional firm that has chosen to embrace mediation and ADR. I believe my business plan could work for an attorney who has already developed a leadership position within the firm or is recognized as a leader in her or his practice area, but probably not otherwise."

SHOULD YOU JOIN A PANEL?

This book primarily talks about solo practitioners and small partnerships rather than panels because, in all honesty, that is my bias. I am convinced that if your goal is to get to the top of the pyramid, going it on your own is the best way. Recently, I was contacted by an organization that was creating a Web site for neutrals, sort of like an online panel. It was not an un-intriguing idea, but it brought me back to the reason I had decided to go it alone in the first place: I didn't really know who these people were, and it would not serve my reputation to attach my name to less well known and possibly less skilled mediators. Highly successful mediators stand apart from the pack: I want people to think of me as really special, not as a commodity that is easily interchangeable with any other mediator on the market.

Many of my colleagues agree with this point of view, but a good number of them don't. In fact, some of the top mediators who contributed to this book run ADR firms or work for them, and a few credit panels with giving them the push they needed to get to the top. And, as Ralph Williams points out, you have to make a name for yourself as a mediator even to be considered to join a panel. "All the provider does is give you another tool in your marketing toolbag. No provider will take you unless you have a practice already."

Panels, or ADR providers, function like brokers for mediators. The advantages of joining a panel are that you can get overflow business, you have use of good facilities, and it handles the business end for you. This can be a great solution for mediators who would rather be mediating than focusing on marketing themselves, and who have enjoyed working in a law firm or other corporate environment.

Alan Brutman, who founded Judicate West in 1993, says, "The reason mediators want to come to Judicate West is our experience in developing huge followings for many talented mediators. Everybody wants to hook up with a provider to seek instant business and credibility from a much larger client base. As a top provider, we have the opportunity, as a result of many years of service and great client relationships and loyalty, to recommend one of our panel members to a lawyer who asks, 'Who's your newest rising star?' That's tremendous credibility for somebody just getting started.

"The number one reason even highly successful mediators would want to join us," he continues, "is the luxury of not having to run a business. We're full-time running a business. When you're a mediator, you want to be mediating twenty hours a day and sleeping four if you could. That means you have to hire someone to run your business, you have to trust that person, and put your career in their hands. . . . There are a lot of headaches that come along with running a business."

Ralph Williams, a successful mediator and member of ADR Services, is in enthusiastic agreement. "I charge a substantial hourly rate, and I give a percentage of that to the house. For that I get a fabulous conference facility, staff, coffee, tea, donuts, Internet. . . . They do all the scheduling, case management, billing and collection, and marketing and advertising. And the house takes the collection risk. It's worth it to me in spades!"

For many entrepreneurial mediators, however, the downside to being a panel member is the potential of becoming a commodity; being on a panel might ultimately reduce your net worth because you're not able to present your own character to the public. Says Robert A. Creo, "Panel members are ultimately people who will compete with you, either internally or externally. I'd rather fill my

Seven Partners

Our business model is unique: seven mediators—we share a common calendar and coordinators. We share expenses. We designed a unique first-class facility, Lakeside Mediation, which has developed its own reputation. Our direct overhead is surprisingly small. We have no debt. We have a managing mediator who is fiscally responsible.

In five years we have not had a single fight about anything. We are friends and part of something we know is special. We are content, happy, and glad to be called mediators.

Eric Galton

own personal calendar and turn business away rather than worry about where panel members are going."

Alan Brutman disagrees strongly with the idea that panel members run the risk of commodification. "We go out of our way not to brand our panel, which makes us attractive to a lot of the independent talent. All of our people are individual talents, and it's up to us to explain and promote their individual attributes to clients."

Some entrepreneurial mediators, such as Cliff Hendler, achieved success by running a panel. "I have a panel of eight or nine people who work for me," he explains. "I'm the rainmaker; I bring in most of the work. I pay for the advertising and the office space, and I give people everything they need. They get a percentage of their billings. We do all of the arranging, the scheduling—it's easy for them. Most of them work in the office. They eat what they kill: if they're not working, they're not getting paid. I don't expect them to go out and market, although if they do, that's great."

YOUR WORKPLACE

As should by now be abundantly clear, successful mediators work long hours—and we don't always have the luxury of working on our home turf. I feel very fortunate to have my own mediation center, with large conference rooms and separate caucus rooms, and I have enough business that this kind of overhead makes sense. Nonetheless, I can't always bring my cases to my own workplace. I have to be as comfortable working behind the steering wheel or in the window seat of an airplane or in the business center of a hotel in a city I don't live in as I am in my office.

"The best of all worlds," says Robert A. Creo, "would be to be able to have your mediation center when you need it, and travel to the client when you need to. But to be centrally located and have enough conference rooms is expensive. If you increase your overhead, you have to increase your billing. I'd rather put the extra money into people. That means I travel to a lot of my work." He makes the most of off-site "offices": "If I have to talk on the phone, how can I most efficiently do that? While I'm driving between cases. When I have to write an article, I do it in the airport when I'm waiting for a plane."

Still, it's good to have a place you can call home. As is true of nearly every aspect of this business, however, every mediator puts his or her unique spin on the concept of work space

"My business is a proprietorship; my business is in my home, and my wife looks after my calendar. I'm out of town more often than I'm in town," says Rick Weiler.

Joe Epstein shares an office with a nonmediator in an allied profession. "I think that exposure helps both of us," he says. "Our client bases are different, but sometimes my clients can benefit from his

Sharing a Suite with Lawyers

I'm in a suite I share with lawyers who are not mediators. I've been with some of them almost twenty-five years. We run our own separate practices.

Right now I'm stand-alone. Our profession is a solitary one, although we're really only a phone call or an email away from other mediators. We don't have to deal with our problems in a solitary way. So even though I practice as a solo, I'm not alone. Organizations like the IAM have tempered that. Still, there's a certain value in being able to walk down the hall in the middle of a mediation and get some immediate feedback from another mediator. I follow a solo model now, but it's subject to changes.

Paul Monicatti

---

services, and there are times he introduces me to potential new clients and new sources."

No Desk, No Office, No Clutter

I agree with my colleague who said, "The biggest mistake that anyone can make is starting out with a huge capital expenditure or committing to an expensive overhead arrangement." I would take that one step further: you can actually function quite well as mediator without even having a desk.

I consider my mediation center invaluable to my practice, but I don't have an office or a desk there to call my own. Here's my thinking: my free time is valuable. If I don't have a case, I don't want to

Getting Past Desk Withdrawal

Most mediators like me, who started as attorneys, still think of themselves as attorneys and operate their mediation business as if they were still practicing law: "I have a desk, I have an office, I go to the office and handle my paperwork . . ." I've followed Jeff's lead in doing away with my desk—and not having a desk makes a big difference! You wake up in the morning and say, "I don't have a desk to sit at or phones to answer or paperwork to push. What will I do to be productive?" It's what I often refer to as desk withdrawal, but it forces you to look at your plan and ask, "Which strategy will I employ today? How will I market myself today?" It's all about making every day productive,rather than *thinking* you're being productive because you're sitting behind a desk.

Mariam Zadeh

spend any time in the office. So my mediation center has become an environment only for managing cases. If I have to do email or write letters, I do it at home in my private study, where I have the freedom to do it at my own pace with all the comforts of home.

It's important to understand the power of giving up the clutter that usually surrounds our offices and desks. This clutter includes everything from folders and newspapers and Post-its to the Internet and email and games and the siren call of Web surfing. All these can prevent you from focusing on what you need to do.

So I recommend a radical course: get rid of your desk! I received this valuable advice about ten years ago from Dan Sullivan, a strategic coach in Canada, and it has served me well. Living without a desk doesn't prevent you from doing your work—not with laptops, BlackBerries, and cell phones at your disposal. With fewer distractions, you can concentrate more deeply on your real work and actually accomplish more. This kind of focus, even when it comes to something as seemingly inconsequential as a cluttered desk, will serve you well in your aim for the top.

Your "Props" Tell a Story About You

Mediation is a very personal career. Often we are privy to the most painful details of people's lives, and we achieve an odd kind of intimacy with people who entered as strangers to us. It seems only right to me that we should share something of ourselves. Hence, I make sure that my mediation center is well supplied with what I call my props. And, it seems, I'm not alone.

"We've got a fairly small boardroom, and it's decorated fairly traditionally," says Rick Russell, "but I have some cultural objects that are there because they remind me of something really neat I've done: a piece of coral from a mediation I did in the Bahamas, a soapstone sculpture of a musk ox from Baffin Islands, Nunavut . . . when I see them they make me feel good. The things in my office typically are a bit of a prop that contains a story. My motto is, 'He who dies with the best stories wins.' I'm not so interested in showing off the size of my office or my car. I get to do neat stuff—that's what I brag about. If I can put something in a room that causes people to ask me to tell them about it, and I get to tell them, I'm happy."

I couldn't agree more. As I mentioned earlier, when I was practicing law I felt compelled to make sure my office decor was bland and impersonal so as not to offend clients. Ironically, the only person who was offended was me—I succeeded admirably in creating a working environment that was the antithesis of everything about me that was real. The paintings on the wall had been chosen to match the drapes, not because I particularly liked them. In fact, they made so little impression I can't even remember what they were. If you were to judge me by what you could glean from that office, you'd come away thinking I was a by-the-book fellow with few interests outside of work. In fact, my office was expressing the *inau*-thenticity—for me—of the career path I was then following.

Today I take great joy in coming to work, in part because I am surrounded by objects that express my passions. Among the first things I see every day is an autographed Bob Dylan guitar hanging on the wall and a panoramic photo of the Old Course at St. Andrews. These mementos of music and golf remind me that there's more to life than work. It makes me happy to see these items, and they also offer something individual and interesting to clients.

I sometimes think of this as having props in my office that create an environment of safety and hope. Leaning up against a wall is a well-worn baseball bat with my name and birthday on it. Most people naturally pick it up and ask jokingly what I use it for—beating recalcitrant clients into shape? I welcome these kinds of comments as icebreakers. They naturally bring humor to a tense time, help me make personal connections, and open up discussion.

Opportunities to provide comfort and convenience are all over the place. Bottled water, soft drinks, good coffee—everything that makes people feel at home. These amenities are there for me, because they make me feel good, but I have them for strategic reasons as well.

My props may not speak to the interest of every lawyer and client who sits down to talk with me, but I no longer worry that my affinity for baseball or golf or rock and roll will offend someone else. I am comfortable letting these items help create a picture of me as a real person with a real life. The unspoken message is that if I feel comfortable sharing something of myself with the client, then the client can feel more comfortable opening up a painful part of his or her life to me and entrusting it to my care.

Clients may even decide to trust me because, like them, I enjoy baseball or golf or Bob Dylan—or because, even though they prefer smooth jazz and tennis, my willingness to put myself out there to be known inspires their trust that I'll always be straight with them.

Two Partners and an Associate

Originally, I wanted to run my business with a business partner and have associates, like satellites around a planet. But it's very difficult to market associates—basically, people call because of their experience with *you*. So the panel tailed off fairly quickly. Now three of us work in association: one does primarily family and workplace mediation, with facilitation on the side; one does primarily commercial and workplace mediation, with facilitation and training on the side; and one does equal amounts of training and commercial mediation, with facilitation on the side. So we all sort of do everything and can hand off work from time to time. We don't use many people out of this core.

Rick Russell

YOUR BUSINESS IS YOUR PEOPLE

Everyone who calls my office knows my assistant. That's because for the last ten years she's been my only full-time employee. She handles scheduling and convening, answers the phone, and generally represents me to the world. We don't even live in the same city—she takes the train in every Monday morning at six, stays in her condo near the office, takes the train back on Thursday, and works at home Thursday afternoon and Friday. It's an arrangement that works well for both of us. And, as you'll see in the next chapter, I consider her role one of the keys to my success.

Somebody's always at the mediation center—when I'm at work, I'm never alone. I also employ a talented and multifaceted young man who works part-time as my bookkeeper and as an all-around assistant and receptionist. He also has experience with computers, which has proven to be very helpful in my practice—he helped design my Web site. Another part-time employee began working with me as an extern in high school and recently graduated from college. She does all the paperwork on my cases—sending out notices and bills, maintaining and ordering supplies, and sometimes answering the phone.

Think carefully about your staffing needs. Often, people enter mediation from another career—be it law, social work, insurance, or another field—where they are used to having the full spectrum of office support. "When I was in a structured law office environment, you had a secretary, a file clerk . . . for a mediation business, it seemed like a waste of services," says Michelle Obradovic. "It's a better service to do my own intake. After all, people want to talk to *me* about the issues, the case problems."

The concept of low overhead is a driving force for many successful mediators. "I don't even have a secretary anymore," Obradovic continues. "I have four staff people who do whatever needs to be done and make sure the parties have what they need—get their food, get their faxes—and I fend for myself. I think it's more important to have my parties taken care of than to pay for a staff person to do my convening work. It's a service-oriented business. It's very hospitable."

Paul Monicatti says, "I share a case manager with a nonmediating lawyer in my office. She's here full time—between the two of us—roughly six hours a day for four days, and three hours on Friday. She does scheduling and answers questions about mediation. My support staff is very important to me in a very personal, service-oriented profession like mediation, where personal service is *the* key to success."

"I don't have a staff at all," says Jeff Kichaven. "Everything is done on an independent contractor basis. I use a secretary service for scheduling, billing, and collection. They're off-site. My

From Partnership to Solo Practice

I practiced law from 1970 to 1990, and I was looking for something different. I stumbled across mediation in a two-day training course. The organization that put on the course was using it to find mediators to do a bunch of cases they had. I really enjoyed the course, and did one, two, three cases a month. Over the next two years I thought it would be a positive career direction, and took other courses. I met other mediators. One, Rick Russell, was someone I developed an affinity with. We both decided we would start a mediation firm, Agree, Inc.

The business plan was to offer a full range of ADR services, including mediation, training, and design, because the commercial mediation market in southern Ontario was not such that you could make a living from it.

We wanted to target a particular market, and we thought we could successfully target the upper end—the largest law firms, charter banks, provincial and federal government. Within a year we had secured consulting work for both the federal department of justice and a major Canadian bank. The legal community heard about our success in these markets, which raised our stock. We got busier and busier.

But by 1997 I knew I wanted to do mostly commercial mediation, so I left Agree and set up as a sole practitioner. At that time the market was changing, and Ottawa had developed an early court-mandated mediation program. I was acceptable to the lawyers up there because I was from out of town. I did more and more cases there, and after a year I moved to Ottawa and the practice flourished—I was mediating every day.

Rick Weiler

bookkeeping is done by an independent contractor who has a number of professional clients. There's almost no filing or secretarial work. I'm a subtenant in an executive suite, so the people who sort the mail are employees of my landlord. It's really an elegant business operation. I have what I need, I don't pay more than I need to get it, I control most of it myself, and I have good relationships with the people I work with. It's a nice way to run a business."

"Keeping overhead down is key," says one successful mediator. "Be self-sufficient. I have a good friend who is a fabulous legal secretary, and I call her when I need help. I have an office downtown, but I do all my own scheduling and billing in my office at home. A staff would be $60,000 a year. My costs are really under control. My overhead is less than 10 percent of my gross."

"My office manager is off-site, and she manages the practice," says one top mediator. "I have other part-time assistants. One is a panelist who is co-owner and a lawyer—and who is also my wife. She takes care of the business aspects, and the other people are more administrative."

"You have to think about what model of support staff you're going to use," advises Robert A. Creo. "Are you going to be in a small group and share the cost of staff support? It's important when somebody calls your office that they get immediate service. When we're actually working mediations, it's impossible for us to service two places at once. You need a human being to answer your phone and be responsive, so that if people want a date and want information there's someone there to do that. I have two administrative assistants who work full time, Monday through Friday. They're not lawyers or paralegals. One does all the bookkeeping and scheduling and phone answering; the other one does the Web page update and other functions. Either one can answer phones and get basic information and respond to queries immediately, because I have case forms and infrastructure for all that."

NOT YOUR ORDINARY CAREER

Writing this chapter, I was struck by how personal mediation is as a profession. Despite the fact that mediation has given a home to so many lawyers fleeing from the world of advocacy, our concerns have much in common with social workers, therapists, and others who provide services to people in crisis. Like any businessperson, we do need some sort of business plan. And of course we need the requisite accountants, insurance agents, support staff, and others to help us run our business. In almost every way it is important for our business to express something of ourselves, our interests, our personalities, our passions. (By the same token, even though you're keeping your overhead low, a premium investment of money and care in your staff will return much more in bookings because of the sincere concern a dedicated staff has for your well-being.) This aspect of a mediator's business connects with clients where it counts: on the personal level. I believe that being able to express your uniqueness in everything you do—including how you decorate your workplace and think about your staff—is a key ingredient in raising yourself above the scores of mediators who are beginning a practice as you read these words.

TOP-TIER STRATEGIES

1. Choose a business model that fits your style.

Every business model has an upside and a downside: provider groups offer institutional acceptance and staff to do the scheduling and marketing, but they can also dilute the value of your name by subsuming you in the organization. The boutique approach, where a few mediators share overhead, can be helpful—but only if the people you are working with do not fear their partners as competitors. Collaboration works when the people involved are not jealous of one another, but partnering just for the sake of having a partnership is a waste of vital time and resources. Do it only if there is economic value in the relationship. If you already know you're entrepreneurial and enjoy meeting and greeting, there's no need to join with others: you already understand that the only person responsible for generating business is you.

2. Make a plan.

Many people who become mediators do so because they love mediating, but they are not businesspeople and don't know much—if anything—about business plans. It's imperative to make some sort of plan for yourself, whether it's the goal tracking we discussed in this chapter or an operating plan of your own choosing, and to review it periodically. Without a plan, it's easy to get discouraged. With a plan, you can see that you really are on track toward your goal.

3. Consider your surroundings.

Mediation is personal. When your work environment expresses something of who you are as a person, it creates a connection with clients and parties that carries over into the mediation room. Make sure clients and parties have everything they need to feel comfortable when they are in your offices.

4. Consider finding a mentor as a fast-track approach to starting a practice.

One of the most valuable things you can do as a new mediator is connect with a mentor whose style and practice you admire. The benefits to you can be great: inside knowledge you don't get in the classroom, and the opportunity to make contacts and have a champion at your side. Strive to make the relationship beneficial for both of you.

5. **Consider mentoring as a way to share your knowledge and segment your market.**

Acting as a mentor not only is the right thing to do but also can give you a whole new perspective on your work. Another bonus is market segmentation: you can open up work in areas you may have outgrown, reaping financial benefits and keeping clients who might have gone elsewhere.

6. **Keep your staff to a minimum and treat them well.**

If you are in private practice as a mediator, keeping your overhead low is primary, but don't skimp on your staff's salary. The most important office support is a friendly, knowledgeable person who is always there to answer the phone and act as your agent when clients need information or want to schedule a case. The person handling your calendar can have a great impact on your success, so choose him or her carefully.

6

How Much Money Can You Earn?
Value, Investment, and Cold, Hard Cash

Making money as a mediator is no secret. It's value for service. If the clients feel that they are receiving value, the fees are not an issue.

Gary Furlong

How much money *can* a talented full-time entrepreneurial mediator earn? Let's reframe that statement: "I'm going to give you 100 percent of my focus," says Rod Max. "What is that day worth?"

A select few mediators at the top of the field, who practice in profitable niches and work in favorable markets, currently command up to $10,000 per day; a small number of mediators nationally and internationally earn $1 million or more per year. Other top mediators, with just as much talent, may make half or even one-third that amount, yet still be at the top of the range for their region. How much money *you* can earn in your mediation practice will depend on several factors: your market niche and client base, your location, your skills, your ability to market yourself effectively, how you value yourself and your time and your money, how you run your business . . . and, significantly, how you set your fees. "You want to be reasonable, but you also want people to respect the value of your day or hours. Some people try to undercut on fees. I believe you need to pick a value you think is appropriate for your day," says Rod Max.

Here's the bottom line on the bottom line: successful mediators charge more—even for routine cases—because, as we have seen, the perception in the marketplace is that you get what you pay for. Clients who are willing to spend the money for mediation—which, in most cases, will be far less than litigation would cost—are more likely to invest more money in a mediator who they feel will settle the case in a fair and timely manner. As one mediator told us, "I raised my rates so I could work less, but I ended up working more!"

IF YOU WANT TO MAKE MONEY, CHOOSE A PROFITABLE NICHE

"Mediation is a place to make money," says Rod Max. But it's not easy. "How many people around the country are making $250,000, $500,000 a year? We have a few who earn $500,000, and there are fewer as you go up the line. When you get up to $1 million per year or more, there are maybe a handful."

Most of the mediators who are earning the big money entered mediation from a career as attorneys or judges, and mediate litigated cases. These kinds of complex high-stakes cases involve dollar amounts that few mediators who specialize in community dispute resolution or small-estate divorce cases can ever hope to achieve. It's hard to argue with the assessment of Ralph Williams that "the universe divides into two parts: mediators who used to be judges, and mediators who used to be lawyers. Nobody who isn't a former judge or a former lawyer is making any money. I suppose it's theoretically possible that somewhere in the United States someone who used to be a therapist is making money, but it's not likely." (Of course, there are always exceptions to the lawyer-only rule, notably Bernie Mayer, who was drawn to dispute resolution from a social services background, and Cliff Hendler, who began in the insurance industry and is now president of DRS Dispute Resolution, one of Canada's largest providers of ADR services.)

A Turnkey Operation?

Mediators who work through providers can make as much money as people out there on their own. The superstars are going to make their money no matter what. There is seven-figure potential at a provider. The key is that you're getting maximum volume of work and exposure without the overhead. The bottom line is, a percentage of your hourly rate is going to go to running the business—marketing, ads, employees, office expenses, and so on. To the majority of mediators, it makes good sense to affiliate with professional ADR providers like us and have a turnkey operation.

Alan Brutman

Particularly in the case of retired judges, there is a certain amount of built-in trust and respectability—even if their skills in facilitating and closing deals aren't always optimal. But a big reason that former lawyers and judges earn well is that the kinds of cases and clients where the financial exposure is greatest naturally gravitate to them: class action, construction defect, malpractice, mass tort, and so on. As we've seen, lawyers are the gatekeepers for most cases—and when the stakes are high, they are generally more comfortable with mediators who they feel know and understand the law.

These cases also tend to be worth more money by their very nature. Generally, you can charge far more for class action and mass tort cases because the return on investment for the lawyers is substantial, and the mediator's fee is a drop in the bucket compared to the risk and reward. You can make money on construction defect cases because they tend to be drawn-out affairs in which the mediator serves more as a litigation manager or special referee. You can charge more for multiparty cases because a lot of people are contributing and splitting the pot. And in large business disputes between Fortune 500 companies, lawyers actually *want* to go to the mediator who charges the most. Why? So that if the case goes south for some reason, they can point to the expensive and well-known mediator and tell their client that they gave it their best shot!

IF YOU WANT TO MAKE MONEY, WORK IN A PROFITABLE MARKET

Mediation markets vary with geography. Canada is different than the United States in general, and different states have widely varying markets. Texas and Florida were originally great places for mediators, but now the market is saturated with them and has leveled off. I was fortunate to be in Los Angeles when the market was in its infancy, and helped serve as a catalyst to lawyers in developing the market. Being a pioneer has its advantages.

"Certain issues in specific parts of the country are more amenable for people using mediation," says Chris Moore, "especially places where you get court referrals. For example, family practice or commercial practice in states that require mediation prior to going to court are easier locales to get cases than where mediation is totally voluntary. In places where there is not institutional support for mediation, it takes longer to build a climate and culture that encourages the use of mediators. My colleagues and I found this to be the case in Colorado in the early days of mediation. We found that it was hard to support ourselves by working in Colorado alone, so we went national and international. This helped build a good client base and ultimately has helped us find new opportunities in our home state."

Just as people who live in Los Angeles and New York tend to earn more (and have a higher cost of living) than people who live in Utah or Nebraska or Ohio, mediators in densely populated parts of the country tend to be able to charge more for their services. For example, a mediator in Los Angeles can easily charge almost twice as much as a mediator in Indiana. A really good year for a top-tier mediator in Pittsburgh might be $500,000, whereas in Los Angeles it might be approaching $1.5 million.

The laws regarding mediation also have something to do with the market. States where mandatory mediation is in effect generally have lower rates because the market is inundated with mediators. For example, many jurisdictions have local court rules that mandate the use of mediation in most civil cases. When the lawyers are scheduling their cases, they now include an effort at sitting down with a mediator before the case gets to trial. Other jurisdictions depend on the attitude of the judiciary. Most judges have now been fully educated in their respective markets about the value of referring cases to private mediators and are encouraging lawyers at early status conferences to seek out a mediator. Pepperdine has spent a number of years providing extensive workshops and training primarily to the Center for Judicial Education and Research (CJER), which has raised the awareness of judges throughout California about the use of mediation. At the same time, however, this effort has also catapulted many judges out of the judiciary into private practice because of their ability to make more money as mediators than they ever could as judges. These market forces have now created their own momentum, creating the perception that the first choice of litigators tends to be retired judges, though seasoned and educated purchasers of mediation services have actually gravitated toward the professional skilled mediator.

Other countries have looked to the United States for direction in developing their own mediation programs, and we have seen a maturation in the marketplace. This has resulted in more cut-rate "providers" who are competing for their piece of the dispute pie and offering discounts to large purchasers. The impact of this "commodity effect" is to drag prices downward. It also highlights the inherent tension between those mediation groups that are focused on quantity versus mediators whose focus is on quality.

IF YOU WANT TO MAKE MONEY, SET YOUR FEES AGGRESSIVELY

My fees are high. I set my fees aggressively, basing them on my years of experience and skill as a closer. And this strategy has served me very well.

Your pricing strategy will depend on your market and how you see yourself in your market. If your goal is to do volume personal injury cases, then you will likely be viewed as a commodity—there are a lot of mediators offering this kind of service—and lower prices will give you a competitive advantage. We see this in many industries. In personal computers, for instance, Dell has dropped its prices dramatically to compete with HP, Gateway, and IBM, and people have begun to see their products as interchangeable and expendable. You can make a decent living competing in a commodity market like this, but you will never reach the top tier or draw the most complex matters.

Pricing aggressively can be a winning strategy, and top-tier mediators almost uniformly tend to put their fees very far along the high end of the continuum. "Pricing strategy is a beauty contest," says one. "If you charge rock-bottom prices, those prices will devalue your service. Parties want to know why your prices are so low. My view is to charge the maximum the market will bear."

Perhaps paradoxically, higher fees can be good for everybody. "Here in Alabama," explains Michelle Obradovic, "an aggressive fee strategy is one of the ways we help the market. We don't have mandatory mediation; we don't have rules, state certification, or regulation. We try to make sure that the new people who want to get into this business get low-cost, quality training and have a mentor relationship, and we help bring them in. So for a very limited time, six months, they do pro bono and low-cost mediation. Then we get them to the $200 per hour level as soon as possible. This raises the level of the market for all of us. We're all sort of working together to raise the standard and market level."

You Have to Say, "My Time Is Valuable"

I believe the best way to be successful is to do a model of flat billing where you're not tied to hourly rate. The other advantage is to bill in advance and get paid in advance. That way you've got their money, and you don't have a cash flow problem. You get the people committed, and you don't spend time billing people or collecting money, you get people who are serious about mediation, and you establish yourself as a high-end in-demand mediator. You have to be strict about cancellation fees once they've confirmed the date. There's a lot of resistance on this from mediators who think they'll lose the competitive edge, but you have to say, "My time is valuable, and these are my rules."

Robert A. Creo

Robert A. Creo says, "I've made a conscious decision to segue into the higher end of the market. I use a per diem–per party approach. For example, if I have a five-party case, they each pay me $1,500 per day, so my billing is $7,500 per day. If I spend six hours on the mediation, I am able to make $1,000 an hour."

"In order to make money, *you* have to mediate," says Cliff Hendler, who runs a panel of mediators. "You can't rely on your panel to make you a lot of money. I charge a lot of money—$5,000 a day. I price myself out of the smaller-end market. I concentrate on bigger cases. And it works—people pay it."

Rick Weiler works primarily in Ontario, where "mandatory court-connected cases are done for a capped fee. At a certain point I said, 'I'll do those cases, but at a market rate.' I've tried to make sure that my fees are competitive, but raise them as the market permits. As a consequence, my wife and I make a very comfortable living."

YOU'RE IN CHARGE OF
HOW YOU SET YOUR FEES

Not surprisingly, how you charge—and what you feel your time is worth—are crucial factors in how much money you can make. If you apologize for your fees or feel guilty when you bill your clients, you may be happy in some ways, but chances are good that you are not going to be among the top fee generators in the profession. You don't have to be afraid to negotiate your fees. As one mediator told us, "Why should I be afraid to negotiate about my rates? I'm in the business of negotiation."

There are any number of ways to bill clients, and you will find the one that suits you and your client list best. Most mediators have experimented with various forms over the years. My own motto is, keep it simple. For example, I prefer not to do hourly billing because it becomes complicated. I generally bill by the day, and I send out a bill in advance of the case. Everyone pays, and we don't have to chase our money. Sometimes the case finishes early, and I get to play golf in the afternoon. Sometimes it goes until midnight, and I sleep only a few hours that night. It all balances out, and in balance this system works very well. I generally don't charge for the petty things, like reviewing briefs and follow-up telephone calls, except under extraordinary circumstances.

There's no "right" way. One of Alabama's most successful mediators, Rod Max, calls his thinking about fees an "evolution." He says, "Some people charge daily, some charge hourly. I went from per party per hour to per party per day, and now I'm charging a flat hourly rate. Originally, I varied the rate depending on the number of parties: it made for a lower amount for more people, but the base number went up. If you have three people at $140 you're making $420 per hour. But that got confusing, so I took it to per party per

Negotiating the Allocation

In some large multiparty cases, before we can even begin, the first thing we do is a mediation among the parties on how they will finance the process: all the parties have to decide how they are going to share the payments and resources. First they talk individually, then they come together and reach an agreement. Usually, if they're ready to go, they'll figure out a way to allocate resources for a dispute resolution initiative.

Chris Moore

day. But that was limiting. I saw that I was giving up time. So I went to $475 per hour no matter how many parties. But this is the product of an evolution from low hourly rate to per party per hour to per party per day to high hourly rate. In the last three years, I've averaged over $1 million a year."

"I've done various things," says Susan Hammer. "In fact, I recently changed my approach. I decided to bill full days, not half days. I never take a deposit because I trust people. And I rarely get burned—I've lost maybe $1,000 in all these years."

"I charge by the hour," says Steve Cerveris. "I do not charge up front—I bill after the mediation. My collections are not perfect, but my first goal is to get clients in the office and help them resolve their case. It's come back to haunt me a couple times, but my collections are much better as a mediator than they were as a lawyer."

No matter what you charge, make sure you're consistent with *how* you charge—and charge what you're worth. Personally, even if you are consistent, I think it's a mistake to charge different prices for different types of disputes, because it confuses the marketplace.

However, many of us do that because we recognize that the marketplace is willing to pay higher prices for certain types of disputes. The best practice is to charge the same thing for all disputes without concern for the complexity of the dispute. Although you might lose market share in some areas, you're likely to gain respect and market share in areas where litigants are not concerned with price.

Some may choose to charge according the type of project. "We are a fee-for-service nonprofit," explains Chris Moore. "The majority of our clients and the disputes that we mediate involve either government agencies or nonprofit or situations where government entities, the private sector, and public interest groups come together to fight. Often our work in the corporate sector also has to do with businesses' interaction with public or government agencies. Regarding fees, some of our projects are charged by the hour, others by the day, and still others by the projected total cost of the intervention. We often charge in phases. If we're mediating a fairly complex dispute, we first do an assessment, talk to all parties, develop an outline of all the issues and opportunities and barriers, and develop a proposal with a budget for a collaborative decision making or dispute resolution process. So the situation assessment costs x dollars, and the convening process costs y dollars, and the meetings cost z dollars.

"Sometimes we do a whole-process contract," he continues, "estimating a number of meetings. For example, if we know we need three plenary sessions with fifty people, and sixteen technical working group meetings to work on details, and each of these meetings will be of two days in duration, we can estimate preparation, meeting time, follow-up, and travel time. Then we negotiate a lump-sum contract based on our estimated amount. On occasion we do a not-to-exceed contract or negotiate a trigger for when we need to talk with the parties if the process will be longer or more expensive than we originally projected."

Even with a contract, however, Moore's firm remains flexible. "Sometimes we do a contract and go back and negotiate for addi-

Name Your Price

With my best repeat users, I have an arrangement whereby they can ask me to mediate any matter on their desk and name their price. That means that they can mediate those matters that would normally not sustain my daily charge-out rate but nevertheless need to be mediated (as litigation sure isn't an option if it can't be mediated at a commercial rate)—I make it very clear that I am doing this as a service *for them* rather than their clients . . . how they paint it with their clients is up to them. (I hope that they take the kudos.) I have never had this arrangement abused, and I have always been paid a fair price for the service I provided.

Geoff Sharp

in excess of two hours (usually a half-day or full-day session), then I charge them for the full time they have blocked (even if they settle early) because they have requested that I block a substantial period of time exclusively for them. In both situations, I do not schedule the next mediation until the clients have paid in full for their last session."

Jeff Kichaven bills on a full-day basis—one rate for less complex cases and a higher rate for more complex cases that have more than three sides. "The day includes one hour of prep time and eight hours on the mediation day, payable in advance. That way nobody accuses me trying to drag out the mediation in order to earn more fees." Mediators can, to some degree, control the pace and timing of the negotiation. "I charge per hour for overtime. If the mediation goes over by fifteen minutes or a half hour, it's more of a hassle to bill

How Much Money Can You Earn?   14

tional time. Or a client may want a running record and they add on, based on progress being made. It depends on the case and what the client is comfortable with. We have a discussion of how a budget would work."

Customs and practices regarding how to charge also vary regionally. "The per diem fee is the way it's done in California," explains Michael Landrum. "I tried it for a long time here in Minnesota and got lots of flak from lawyers who wanted hourly fees. They'd say, 'If we pay you a per diem fee and we settle in two hours, then you made x dollars an hour!' I used to do a lot of multiparty construction cases, and I had a great fee system where it was a per diem charge per party, with discounts for more parties—but they said no, charge an hourly fee."

"I had daily rates at one time for local and travel," says Michelle Obradovic, in Alabama. "My market is oriented toward hourly rates. Everybody I know who switched to daily rates switched back. In other parts of the country they prefer daily rates. I'll still do class action and multiparty when I have to get on a plane. And if I don't get paid in advance, I don't come."

"I charge by the hour or the day, depending on what people want," says Ralph Williams. "I make it easy for them to buy: How do you want to pay? Hourly? Half day? Full day? That's enough choices. My fees fall into the acceptable band of pricing—the upper–middle range between the highest hourly rates and the lowest. If I started charging higher than the acceptable band, I would lose business. If I charged less, people would think something was wrong. I'm happy right where I am."

Nina Meierding's business is 80 percent family mediation and 20 percent other types, including litigated cases, and her fee practices reflect these two very different types of clients. "I charge my clients on an hourly basis, and there is no retainer. They pay at the end of each session for the actual time they have used. Usually, it's a two-hour appointment. However, if the attorneys are also present at the mediation and they wish to block an extended period of time out—and you gain goodwill from people if you write off small amounts. But sometimes you're there late at night, above and beyond the call of duty for a normal day's work. I believe that if it's appropriate for lawyers to charge for this kind of work, it's appropriate for mediators too."

"I charge flat fees based on a two-party base, and then I have a factor for the complexity of the case, the value of the case, and the number of parties," says Joe Epstein, in Colorado. "If there are more parties, I add to the base fee. If there's more at stake and more work involved, I add to the base fee. I do this because I'm in a lower-price market, so my base rate is relatively low. When more is at stake, people are willing to pay more for the added complexity and the increased stakes."

"I have different fee models for local versus out-of-state cases because if I can sleep in my own bed, I don't mind giving a discount," says one mediator. "A pricing strategy is probably the toughest decision to make and the one aspect of my practice that I have the least hard analysis to back up."

THE BEST INVESTMENTS ARE IN PEOPLE AND PLACE

Earning money involves a willingness to let go of market share. For me, that eventually meant thinking about how to best invest my resources and about what financial return I would expect to receive. It came down to two basic areas: the people who worked with me and the environment in which we worked.

Investing in People

When I was a practicing lawyer, I would hire people to do individual tasks—for example, I had a secretary, a paralegal, a researcher. And when I began my business as a mediator, I continued in this direction. And then I had a breakthrough moment: I saw my investment in my business in a radically different way. Instead of looking for a secretary, a bookkeeper, and so on, I would hire *one person* to speak for me to the world at large. This person would act as my agent—convening the cases, scheduling the cases—and would also answer the phone, talk to clients, and simply represent me in the best possible light. That person would also need to have a terrific personality and to enjoy talking to people on the phone.

Admittedly, great people like this are hard to find. They don't have to be perfect at all the tasks, but they do have to have the very best attributes of a salesperson: they must believe in their product (you) and do everything they can to support you, and they have to enjoy people and get along with them in even the most trying of circumstances.

To find and keep these special people, you have to invest in them. My epiphany came when I really began thinking about how I wanted to invest my money in my business. If I invested $40,000 in the stock market, I would have no guarantee of return and no control over performance. In fact, I'd be delighted if I got a 7 percent return on my investment.

Then I realized that if I took that $40,000 in before-tax dollars and paid it to someone in twenty-six biweekly salary installments, I'd have high control over performance and could realize as much as a 150 percent return on my money!

Eventually I found the person I was looking for. And instead of viewing my assistant as a secretary who just does task work for $40,000 a year, I pay her as a professional who gets paid a bonus based on her productivity, and so has a stake in the outcome of the business. Her income is commensurate with a six-figure lawyer's income because she provides tremendous value to the business. When I look at my rate of return, I'm overjoyed. If I had that $40,000-a-year person who was just an order taker, my bookings would undoubtedly be down by 40 percent. I could easily lose hundreds of thousands of dollars a year in lost bookings. But my assistant doesn't just answer the phone; she works at keeping me booked, because she believes in what we do and is personally invested in keeping the business moving forward—think of the rate of return

Making a Ton of Money Is Not My Only Goal

I'm not a ruthless businessman or a bottom-line thinker. I encourage my staff to take a day off with pay each month and do some volunteer work they wouldn't ordinarily do. I've taken my staff on cruises and vacations. Making a ton of money is part of my business, but it's not my only goal. I could be more coldhearted and businesslike and make more money. So I don't make as much money off my staff as I could.

Cliff Hendler

when someone who works for you is affected by the growth of the business!

I have to create the business, of course, but my assistant ensures that business gets booked. So I'm more than willing to invest in a top person. I've had the same assistant for more than ten years, and our arrangement has worked out beyond my wildest dreams.

Investing in Your Environment

I also make it a point to invest in my environment. My mediation center has a couple of large conference rooms and two private caucus rooms to accommodate parties during mediation, and I make sure every chair I purchase for my office is comfortable. I might spend an extra $15,000 on furniture, but I get it back because people appreciate the comfort. It sends a symbolic message of caring, and that helps them want to come back. I see a direct correlation between investing in my environment—and my clients' comfort—and getting a return in terms of business.

This kind of investing does not mean spending wildly. "I am not afraid to spend money on my business," says Michelle Obradovic, "but I make every dollar count. I personally live well below my means because it gives me the most flexibility in my business. In my mediation center, lunch is part of my overhead. The parties get to have menus and pick what they want—sandwiches, pasta salads. We have a little cookie oven, and right after lunch you get a plate of chocolate chip cookies. We bought one guy a bag of cheese sticks because he didn't eat carbs. That kind of stuff makes all the difference. To me that's a valuable expenditure of money!"

Eric Galton's partnership owns Lakeside Mediation, a unique mediation center overlooking Lake Austin that has been called "Zenlike." In an article in the *Texas Bar Journal* Greg Bourgeois (the managing member of the firm, which also includes Ben Cunningham) says, "When people walk in here, their entire affect changes. For years, in teaching mediation, we've stressed the importance of the environment in mediation. I don't think any of us realized just how important it is until we opened this center." The conference rooms lead to decks overlooking the lake, and a bakery is right next door. "It sure beats being stuck on the twenty-fifth floor of an office building in an eight-by-eight conference room," says Cunningham.

Sometimes the environmental investment costs nothing but thinking outside the box (or outside the mediation center). Eric Galton recalls a high-conflict mediation that was going nowhere fast. Suddenly, he says, "A picture flashed in my mind. I realized that my left brain was talking to me and I needed to act before my right brain took over. I grabbed my car keys, removed the parties, and said, 'Come with me. We're going for a ride.' One sat in the front seat, one sat in the back. No one asked where we were going. I stopped the car on a shoulder of a major highway. Next to the shoulder were steps and a path leading to Austin's only and most beautiful Buddhist temple. I turned to the parties said, 'This is where you get out. Explore. The journey ends here. I'll be back in an hour or so.'

"I returned an hour later and saw no one in the parking lot. I waited for thirty minutes in the tranquility garden and then walked up the steps. I found them sitting cross-legged against a wall by the steps. I joined them on the floor and said nothing. Finally, one of them advised me that everything was worked out. We sat for a while and then returned to my office to write up the agreement.

"I have tried to process everything that happened that day," says Galton, "but I have given up. The experience was unbelievable and accentuated my belief in the limitless creativity that the process allows—if we only remain open."

CREATE VALUE FOR EVERYONE

Earning at the top end of the scale does not mean grasping for dollars: pro bono cases, as we pointed out earlier, should be an integral part of every top mediator's career. Why? Because we are in a support-oriented business, and being of service to people is our goal. If some cannot afford our services, our being available to help is like an inexpensive marketing investment and is the right thing to do.

The most successful mediators may price their work aggressively, but they also strive to be fair. As Chris Moore says, "We usually provide a logic and rationale for how we charge, so people understand why we bill the way we do. Clients appreciate knowing about our thinking and generally accept our thinking."

"Making money as a mediator is no secret," says Gary Furlong. "It's value for service. If the clients feel that they are receiving value, the fees are not an issue. We price ourselves above midrange in the market because we want to attract clients who are serious about the process and not throwing the file against the wall to see if it sticks.

"Clients respect professionals who know what they're worth," he explains, "so competing on price makes no sense. On top of that, this is not (yet) a commodity field, and it probably never will be. People rarely say, 'I need to find the cheapest brain surgeon,' and they don't look for the cheapest lawyer or engineer either. That means that quality work will always attract fair fees."

So here's the real secret: the key to earning a substantial living as a mediator can't be all about the money. It has to be about creating value for everyone involved.

It's Not About the Money

Money isn't the main reason I'm doing it—if it was, I'd be hustling more. I see a lot of emphasis in our profession on money. There's more and more talk about making money and how you get more business. And there's nothing wrong with that. But it's changed from "We're doing this because it's 'righteous work.'"

I spent a long time doing good; now I'd like to do well. I like what I do, and I'm making a good living; I'm comfortable with what I do. I know a lot of guys making big bucks. I define it as doing work that I like—I turn down cases I don't like. I define it as the freedom and independence of being my own person and doing my own work.

I started out with trying to have a firm, twenty-two people, fancy offices . . . one by one, the people got old and died or left. That's when I decided I don't want to have an empire. I just want to do the work.

Michael Landrum

TOP-TIER STRATEGIES

1. **Choose a profitable niche.**

    Most top-tier mediators—the ones who charge the most, earn the most, and work the most—come from the legal profession and handle complex litigated cases. If your goal is to make money as a mediator, you are unlikely to achieve this goal if your niche is family mediation, small-estate divorce cases, or community disputes. Construction defect, mass tort, and class action tend to pay higher premiums for skilled mediators.

2. Bill fairly but aggressively.

In my experience, aggressive billing is a winning strategy. Charging fees that are too low devalues you and does not help the field as a whole. Charging the very highest, just because you can, is a shortsighted strategy that ultimately serves no one. Study your market, set your fees reasonably, and give yourself a raise periodically. Your time is valuable: charge what you feel your time is worth.

3. Invest in your people and your work environment.

The people you hire to work for you are an important part of your support structure and help sell your services to clients. To find and keep these special people, you have to invest in them. Treat them as professionals and pay them accordingly. Low overhead doesn't mean keeping all proceeds. Similarly, investing in your work environment is another smart use of your resources. If you have even a small mediation center, make sure it has all the comforts of home for your clients—a comfortable chair and a good cup of coffee can be the tipping point.

4. Create value for everyone.

There's a lot to be said for earning a lot of money doing the work you love, but your financial statement is just part of your success. Make sure that you share the wealth, financial and spiritual, with your associates and employees. And be sure to take time to smell the roses.

7

Staying Alive

Weathering the Ups and Downs of a Mediation Practice

*Business is an up and down process. You either accept
that and plan on it, or you get a job. It's that simple.*

Gary Furlong

I ran into my colleague Henry outside Starbucks. "How's business?"
I asked. He shook his head.

"I'm out of the mediation business," he said. "I'm back to litigating full time."

"That's too bad," I said. "I thought you had a real talent for negotiation."

"Thanks," he replied. "I really do enjoy mediating, but the ups and downs of this business were just too much. I like a salary I can count on. But living from mediation to mediation, and wondering if the phone is going ring again . . ."

"Making the transition can be tough."

"Tell me about it!" said Henry. "Even with my wife working full time at her job, it seemed like we were running backwards financially. My income dropped by tens of thousands of dollars. Litigation isn't as much fun, but at least I can count on it." He said wonderingly, "You know, it looks like such a great life from the outside. How in the hell do you guys do it?"

I hear stories like Henry's all the time. Would-be professional mediators are attracted to the practice like bees to honey, but the

The Long View

Everything is cyclical, and it's often difficult to discern a pattern. Some years, everyone wants to mediate before the end of the year. Other years, there is a flurry of mediation activity right before summer begins. I take a long view. I figure that the highs are going to be offset by the lows, and the lows are going to be offset by the highs, and I just keep plugging away. If I have a slow period, I focus on writing, speaking, and marketing efforts. If I'm busy mediating, I just do that.

Jeff Abrams

---

majority of them drop like flies after a year or so of struggle. Income—not enough of it, or the unpredictability of it—is a big factor, but so are the emotional ups and downs that are a given in this business.

You may be the greatest mediator in the world, but it might still take years to establish a successful mediation practice—if you're lucky enough to be in the right place at the right time, skilled enough to settle cases and make friends and champions among the people who can bring you business, dedicated enough to put in the hours it takes to carry off the cases *and* the marketing—and business-savvy enough to make it work. A vital component in creating a successful mediation practice is being able to weather the ups and downs of a career in which you are only as good as your most recent successful settlement.

CYCLES AND SEASONS

"There are times when it's a little slow, and I panic, and then the cycle picks up, and so it goes," says Michael Landrum. As he and other top mediators have learned, to stay alive in this business, you've got to roll with the punches.

You'll never be in this business so long or enjoy so much success that you're immune to the nagging fear that if the phone stops ringing for even one day, it will never ring again. When this happens to me, as it inevitably does, I try to put it in perspective and stay positive, knowing in my heart that the next call will come. After a while, you learn to see the cycles coming. "In the twenty years I've been doing this I have seen the mediation profession go through different cycles," says Paul Monicatti. "It's important to be able to weather the cycles and understand that they're coming."

"My workflow is pretty steady," says Rick Weiler, "but cases slow down in the summer. I've gotten over the phone not ringing—you ride it out. We all have ups and downs in terms of the results. But like a professional ballplayer, you just shake it off and keep going."

If your practice is tied to lawyers and financial markets, these fluctuations can be real issues for scheduling. And it's easy to predict seasonal connections to a downturn in your business. "July is a slow month for mediators," says Michelle Obradovic. "I might have twenty-five people in a mediation, and *somebody* is going to have a family vacation or a conflict, so I can't even schedule the case. December is almost nonexistent for business. Between family holiday commitments and general stress levels, people aren't willing to commit the resources—familywise and timewise—for mediation."

PATIENCE, PERSEVERANCE, PERSISTANCE

Mediators who naively think they can take their careers quickly from zero to sixty are in for a rude awakening. Virtually every mediator who participated in this book stressed the importance of having a track record and pointed out that it generally takes three to five years of continual success and growing recognition to build one. "I've been a full-time mediator for four years," says one young, highly successful practitioner. "In most fields that would not be very long. But in this field, if you can actually make a living at it, people want to ask how you do it."

The answer? Patience, perseverance, persistence, tenacity. Over and over again, top mediators cite these attributes as crucial contributors to their early and continuing success.

"I get a call once a week from somebody who wants to 'pick my brain' about mediation," says Susan Hammer. "The first thing I say is, 'It's great work, but don't give up your day job.' It takes a three- to five-year plan to make this work."

Nina Meierding advises, "Use your time wisely; be clear about priorities. Otherwise, when the downtimes come you get frantic. My first year, I made $600. After four years I was nowhere close to six figures. But I was also thinking, what is my goal? How much time and money am I going to invest before I reach six figures? You have to have an inordinate amount of patience. I haven't had a down month in ten years—it's been a very consistent, solid, respectable six-figure income for ten years."

The hard truth is, most would-be mediators aren't willing or able to make the commitment of time, energy, and personal sacrifice it takes to persevere through the rocky beginnings and hard times every mediator faces and to put in up to five years to move from a five-figure income to a six-figure income. You must be willing to put your finances on the line, accept continual rejection, put up with the struggle, and ride out the hard times. This is difficult enough for single people. When you have a family, a mortgage, and other financial obligations, it's nearly impossible to make the transition into mediation directly, because—especially if you're coming from a relatively high paying profession—your income drops precipitously.

The mediators who are most in demand are the survivors—the ones who made the cut. Those mediators not only understand what it means to stick to a case until it settles but also know what it means to persevere in service of their own careers.

"You need endurance," advises Meierding. "I combined my legal practice and mediation practice for three years, then cashed in my teacher's retirement and made a commitment to doing mediation full time. I thought, 'If I truly direct my energy to one place, it will work.' And it did."

"Did it take perseverance? You bet it did," says Ralph Williams. "I was managing partner of my own law firm for twenty-five years. Then I tried, from the early 1990s until the mid-1990s, to run a mediation practice in parallel with an arbitration practice, but it was too emotionally, spiritually, and energetically dividing. In 1996, I said I have to stop doing this; and in 1998 I took the plunge. I said, I don't care how much it costs, as long as it doesn't take me more than five years. It took me four years. It was a struggle, but I knew it would take that amount of time. So I never got discouraged, because it was happening at the pace I anticipated it would. If I had left my law firm in 1998 and gone to ADR Services the first year I was recruited (in 2000, instead of 2001), I would have cut a year off."

Perseverance is not something you can fake. "The successful people are extremely invested in the process psychologically and mentally," says Robert A. Creo. "You have to be very committed to what you do, and you have to get intense personal, mental, and emotional satisfaction from it."

Perhaps the most striking story of perseverance occurred during the writing of this book, when Robert Jenks's firm in Metairie, Louisiana, became part of the Hurricane Katrina story of 2005. He told me that this was the most dramatic, profound devastation he has ever seen. Obviously, commerce—and his office—were gone in New Orleans, but he and his partners kept their business together by taking some extra office space in Baton Rouge and working to get the Metairie office back. Their staff pulled together and worked from around the country, online and via phone, to keep cases scheduled and the business on track. "We were scared," said Jenks, "but we tend to run faster when we're scared. There are some speed bumps, but once we affirmatively made the decision to climb the mountain, any obstacles become merely speed bumps and not brick walls—so we know we'll make it to the top."

Persistence and Patience

In time, with a commitment to a good marketing plan and a lot of hard work, for the individual who is trained and also has good leadership and interpersonal skills, the work will come. In order to succeed, one must be both persistent and patient.

Ben Picker

USING THE SLOW TIMES

The phone will not ring every day. Even if your calendar is filled for three solid months, eventually you will have an empty slot. If you're smart, you'll actually learn to welcome these blank spaces in your day as times to work on your business in a productive way.

"I just plan for the slow times," says one top mediator. "I catch up on business filings, interview interns and law students, write a few newsletters or articles, book some speaking engagements, and get ready for what's coming next."

"There have been times when I have honestly wanted more time for my family and myself," says Paul Monicatti. "Actually, I have welcomed some of the downturn in business to allow me to smell the roses and have time for other things in life. This may be even more enriching than just mediating all the time."

Why not just plain enjoy the free days? They are gifts that allow you to recharge your batteries and not think about the business of your profession. In order to be successful you must give yourself time when you're not connected to a cell phone or BlackBerry, and your only "job" that day is to enjoy one of your many hobbies or spend some time with your family or friends. This is just as important as the administrative days when there is no booking on the calendar.

Learning early in your career the art of using free time may actually help you reach your goal more quickly. Mariam Zadeh says, "You need to be aware that you'll find yourself with free time and that you'll have to deal with it. You have to keep yourself motivated. The best thing to do is go back to the business plan you set up and say, 'Hey, I accomplished 1, 2, and 3 on my list!' Then pat yourself on the back and say, 'Now I'll focus on items 4, 5, and 6, and next month I'll focus on 7, 8, and 9.' You always have something to do if you're focused."

Some mediators not only welcome the downtime but even program it into their schedules. "If you're successful," says Ralph Williams, "you have mostly ups and no downs. I choose not to take cases on Friday because I can't bring it to the table five days a week. This work is too hard! When I made the decision not to work on Friday, I was afraid I would lose all I had worked so hard to build. What happened? Nothing. I didn't lose any work. It's an admin and catch-up day."

Susan Hammer also takes time away from mediating. "I try to mediate two or three cases a week," she says. "Because it's so demanding, it's important and fair to clients that I'm rested. I want to give people my best. For me, two or three cases a week generates plenty of income. I spend the rest of my time in leadership roles for nonprofit organizations and with family and friends. I find this level of practice to be sustainable and continually enriching."

"Ask yourself, 'What can I do if I have a gap in this day to give value to the day?'" advises Rod Max. "I find days when I can spend time on the telephone getting people back to the table or prepared to get to the table. In the end, I have more appreciative people who say, 'Rod Max was not only there from nine in the morning until adjournment, he also helped us design a good process and continued afterwards until we achieved resolution.'"

REMEMBER: IT TAKES TIME

By now it should be clear that nobody gets to the top tier overnight or over the course of a year or two. "You have to be willing to give your goal time to ripen," says Zadeh. "For example, suppose your goal is to mediate full time, five cases a week. It might be that in year one, you do three cases a week. In year two you'll move up to four cases a week, and then by year three you've got eight cases a week. A lot of people set high expectations and think that from day one they'll be super busy. It doesn't always happen that way. Sometimes your goals of reaching a certain number of cases per week or month don't work out the way you planned. Along the way, then,

---

Be Engaged in the Process

As a young guy in college, I used to work in a steel mill. When I punched in to work at 7 A.M., I could do those physical, manual duties and get through that day with a minimum of energy. When I punched out at 3 P.M., I never thought about my workday again. As a professional person you don't have that leisure to compartmentalize. Mediator thoughts are always running in and out of your head. Your work is always lingering; it's always around you. If you walk out of a mediation that you haven't settled and you don't feel it in your gut, you're not fully engaged in the process. I believe that mediation has to stay with you a little bit. Every mediation has a good odor or a bad odor that lingers with you. If you don't smell it, maybe you're not engaged. You have to be deep into it.

Robert A. Creo

you may have to alter your strategies and revise your goals. Remember, your career is a work in progress, and your approach must be fluid. Always be willing to deal with the ambiguities."

The key is to stay committed. If you're going to be a successful mediator, you have to commit your time and resources to that goal. "Some people see mediation as a way through retirement," says Rod Max. "For me it's not winding down, but gearing up. The way to get more mediations is to mediate well. I'll start at 7:30 A.M. designing a mediation. By 9 A.M. I begin the day's mediation. Whatever time that concludes, I either travel to the next day's mediation or I follow up on past mediations or prepare for future mediations."

Nina Meierding also stresses the importance of commitment to the primary goal of being a mediator. "Give it respect as to education, capital—be prepared to invest in time, classes, meeting people, changing your office to look like a mediation office. Think about how many years of *not* making money you are willing to put in."

CREATE A FINANCIAL ROAD MAP

If you can stay focused on your goals for a few years and continue to have successes, you will in all likelihood realize your goals. One way to keep yourself from getting discouraged is to create a "financial road map" for yourself. Zadeh suggests graphing your projected gross revenues over a ten-year period. The chart shown in Table 7.1 assumes that experience and exposure to the market will bring steady growth in the number of mediations you conduct per week and the rate you charge per mediation (adjust the numbers to reflect the realities of your own market).

"A graph or chart will make it clear to you how your income can incrementally increase," she advises. "You can also see that as you gain more experience, you'll be increasing your fee. When you see it on paper," she says, "you can see the present risk of making the transition to full-time mediation, and your potential reward down the road. If you're risk averse, underestimate the numbers a little

166 HOW TO MAKE MONEY AS A MEDIATOR

Table 7.1. Ten-Year Revenue Projection Chart.

Years	Mediation Fee per Half Day	Number of Half-Day Mediations per Week	Total
1–2	$1,500	2	$144,000
3–4	$1,500	4	$288,000
5–6	$2,000	6	$576,000
7–8	$2,000	8	$768,000
9–10	$3,000	10	$1,440,000

bit. That way, even if you're not busy every day of the month at the beginning, you'll feel more secure and won't get as easily bruised by the bumpy start."

With the addition of two more columns illustrating how fees will be shared between mentor and mentee (as shown in Table 7.2), this same chart can also be used as a presentation piece to a prospective mentor to demonstrate the financial value of taking you on as a mentee.

Feeling secure about reaching your goal is a key factor in keeping yourself climbing that pyramid. "For about twelve years," says one top mediator, "I was like the rocket being put into orbit from Cape Canaveral. I was putting in a lot of energy, burning the fuel. It was work, work, work. I had to borrow money, go into hock; my revenue was flat, and we were living off the loan. But in the last few years I've gone into orbit—the fuel's been burned, the orbit is steady, I just have to do little course corrections to prevent the orbit from decaying."

You also have to be practical. "Living below my means is self-preservation," says Michelle Obradovic. "I really love this job and don't want to get overextended and go back to my law practice. Getting a super-fancy office, spending a lot on decorators, buying $2,000 designer business suits—that's not going to happen."

"You've got to be in it for the long haul," agrees Paul Monicatti. "In terms of your spending habits, you have to be able to plan for

Table 7.2. Adding Value as a Mentee.

Years	Mediation Fee	Number of Half-Day Mediations per Week	Total	Mentor	Self
1–2*	$1,500	2	$144,000	$50,400	$193,600
3–4*	$1,500	4	$288,000	$100,800	$187,200
5–6**	$2,000	6	$576,000	$194,000	$382,000
7–8**	$2,000	8	$768,000	$242,000	$526,000
9–10***	$3,000	10	$1,440,000	$388,000	$1,052,000

*Based on a mentor and mentee allocation of 65 percent and 35 percent for income between $0 and $500,000. These ratios are, of course, negotiable between mentor and mentee.

**Based on a mentor and mentee allocation of 75 percent and 25 percent for income between $500,000 and $999,999. These ratios are, of course, negotiable between mentor and mentee.

***Based on a mentor and mentee allocation of 80 percent and 20 percent for any income $1 million and over. These ratios are, of course, negotiable between mentor and mentee.

the inevitable down cycle. Turn it around into a positive. That has more value than the loss of business. The increase in available time for family and other important things in life may outweigh the downturn in business."

Stay on Top of Your Trends

Just as the captain of a sailboat must continually be aware of changing currents in order to reach port safely, observing your practice and making necessary course corrections is vital. You may need to tweak your approach to how you set your fees, how you market yourself, or your business model. Even if you feel you've reached the top, it pays to review your business continually. "My practice is always a work in progress," says one successful mediator. "I have a detailed operating plan, as well as a detailed development plan for my business. About every three months, I read both of them word

Value the Up Times

Value the "up" times. Feeling good about yourself, having someone call and say he or she is referring you on a case, having people call you and say you did a great job—when everything comes together like that, it's great. Capture that feeling and hold on to it, because it all weaves together. If you're not being positive, how can you move forward?

Mariam Zadeh

---

for word, start to finish. About every six months, I revise them. During the time in between, I keep a blank journal with me to write notes to myself to read during the review process."

"Trust the process and observe the results," advises Rod Max. "You always have to analyze your practice from calendars to collections to accounts receivable to billing. I do comparisons every year. How many mediations did I have this year, last year? I compare my billings; I compare my collections. Am I working more and enjoying it less? Am I working less and enjoying it more? Could I have billed more? Should I have billed less? This kind of self-critical analysis has to go on as often as monthly, and no less than quarterly, to stay on top of the trends."

DEALING WITH EMOTIONAL OVERLOAD

When you don't settle—or worse, when a few cases in a row don't settle—it's draining. You begin to doubt your worth. You know you've done a lot of good work, and you may have done great work on those cases. But ultimately, you've got to close out these deals. Not getting to closure just saps your energy. As Robert A. Creo says, "The human moments are so powerful and enriching. They make you say, 'I really want to settle this case!'"

"You have to be prepared for the emotional roller coaster," says my associate, Mariam Zadeh. "You're thinking, 'So-and-so will go to bat for me' or 'I'm going to call in this favor and I'll get this case,' and then it doesn't pan out. These are the realities you have to face in the beginning of your career. Some days are disappointing. At first, you look at it philosophically and think, 'Oh, I guess I didn't get this business. Maybe next time.' Often, it just feels like personal rejection."

Mediation as a sole practitioner can be lonely. If you don't have other mediators in the office to bounce ideas off of, especially during times when there is little work coming your way, you can feel very isolated. One way to break out of this to meet with other mediators to discuss ideas of mutual interest. "I've made a concerted effort in the last two years to reach out and join high-quality mediator groups," says one of my colleagues. "I go to conferences twice a year, and I get to do high-end thinking and talking about mediation with high-end people. That's been very valuable for me."

"When you settle case after case after case," says Ralph Williams, "you think you're fabulous. When you don't settle a case, you think you've totally lost your touch. If you're subject to loneliness or depression, this business is not for you. Your emotions magnify because you're alone. You have to have your feet on the ground. I try not to take myself too seriously. I remind myself that everything I have is a gift, and I need to be a prudent steward of it and use it well."

It's important to move through the feelings and be ready, willing, and able to maintain an aggressive follow-up schedule that continually nudges parties closer to their objectives. Call, write, schedule another session. Do everything you can to bring the parties closer, one small step at a time. Because once the parties are closer, they feel more willing to be flexible. (As Tracy Allen says,

Survival Skills

Those of us who get up every Monday morning to sit in the mediator's chair need survival skills, and we all differ as to what does it for us. A real danger for me is being hardened to conflict, and I often reflect about the potential for me to lose my compassion. Even in dollar disputes, a form of compassion and generosity to those in conflict is required to be an effective neutral. Once that is eroded over time, no other mediator skills can compensate, and the market will talk about you being stale, robotic, or worse, burned out. I think I am susceptible to this, and I have seen it in other mediators. But that's the marvelous thing—parties notice everything!

Geoff Sharp

"Blessed are the flexible, for they shall never be bent out of shape!") And have faith in the process: eventually, most cases do settle.

Even when you settle successfully, mediation can be draining. Conflict is never pretty, and it can be exhausting to be the emotional focal point for a room full of angry people. What we do may *look* easy to the untutored, but successful mediators all agree that, contrary to the belief of many would-be mediators, it takes stamina and endurance to do this work. Worse, many cases revolve around terrible traumas and unthinkable losses. "Luckily, I've never experienced burnout," says Paul Monicatti, "but there are periods you go through where many of the cases involve death and destruction, grieving families, high emotions, children confined to wheelchairs or persons in permanent vegetative states. . . . That kind of heartache can gang up on you. A break from that is helpful."

No one can work at full speed day in and day out without needing to find a way to recharge his or her batteries. Over the years, like most other successful mediators, I have developed a few tools for dealing with the emotional and physical toll of intense mediation.

Stay Fresh

Finding ways to stay fresh is a continual challenge. "You stay alive by constantly reinventing yourself as a mediator," says Eric Galton, "acquiring and developing new techniques, hanging out at least twice a year with other mediators, and taking enough vacation time to recharge. Also, maintaining your other passions is critical. I don't feel I compete with other mediators. We collaborate and exchange ideas. We all need to get better at what we do. At least twice a year, I take a hard look in the mirror and ask, 'How can I do what I love better?'"

Michael Landrum concentrates on moving forward. "How do I deal with the ups and downs of the business? One of the keys for me is trying to stay ahead of the curve of types of cases. Different forms of mediation, formats, styles—the whole field is constantly evolving. I change the way I do things. If you want to do this for a living, the way you learned may not be the right way anymore. Figuring out what's next is the continuing challenge. Keep yourself fresh and stay ahead of the field."

Go on education vacations, where you are forced to learn about something you don't know about. This will train your mind to be creative. You can also discuss case evaluations with colleagues, particularly in subspecialties where you have not mediated. Ask other mediators what they might do in a given hypothetical situation, as you will learn a number of different techniques that might not be in your toolbox.

Take Home the Gems

After I play a game of golf, I think back to each of the eighteen holes and look at what I did right, what I did wrong, how I might have played it differently. I take the same approach in my practice.

At the end of every session, I like to look for the learning points, find the gem, and understand what caused the tipping point in the case. That requires a quiet meditation, perhaps with a glass of pinot noir, during which I sort through what happened that day. Inevitably, I will identify at least one moment that is worth remembering.

Another trick is to remember the stories people tell during the sessions, or the narrative of the case itself. These stories are the living, breathing, driving forces that inspire you to keep on doing this for a living. I keep a journal of interesting cases, jotting down interesting quotes and humorous or startling insights and the often wonderful anecdotes that people use. And sometimes I start to incorporate these to expand my own repertoire.

Create Comfort Breaks

I also continually try to come up with different ways to create comfort and value in my environment. For example, I installed cable TV in the mediation center so that we have access to the news when attention and energy flag during a lengthy mediation. I always make sure to have a variety of unique reading materials accessible to people if they need to take a break and get their mind off the process for a while. Perhaps one of the best things I did years ago was to buy an espresso machine for the mediation center. Even if you just decide on the spur of the moment to bring in bagels for the staff, you help energize everyone.

Letting Go

Sometimes, especially after a particularly rough or draining session, you just have to put the day out of your mind and move on. "Some of us deal with highly emotional cases," says Cliff Hendler, "stories you don't want to hear about, let alone think about. Hearing about these things and becoming involved in helping to resolve some of the issues help you grow as a human being and help you be thankful

Get Used to It!

I sometimes compare having a mediation business to running a restaurant. You may have reservations this Saturday night and next Saturday night, but you probably don't have reservations for six months from now. We might have mediations for the next month, but nobody has a contract to give us mediations six months out. In law practice, an individual lawsuit can last for months or years. In mediation, your cases last for a day or a few days—you need new cases coming in all the time. It can be very difficult to get used to. It takes a certain intestinal fortitude to take a long-term view. It's very difficult to keep a stiff upper lip and keep doing the marketing when things are slow. Yet you have to do it. Swim or die.

What's my secret? Get used to it! It's not going to go away.

Jeff Kichaven

---

for what you've got. They make you more humane. But there are cases that haunt you because they're so horrific. You've got let it go—a bathtub memory. When it's over, you pull the plug and let it go."

TOP-TIER STRATEGIES

1. **Accept that there will be slow times and plan for them.**

   It's the law of gravity: what goes up must come down. The trick is not to take the inevitable downtimes personally. Instead of being surprised when you have a gap on your calendar, use that time wisely: work on your marketing, make calls to clients, review your business plan—or just take the day off! The key is knowing in your heart that business will pick up soon, and continuing to work in that direction.

2. Be patient and persistent.

It takes from three to five years to build a solidly successful mediation career. During all that time—whether your practice is going well or not so well—you must be engaged, committed, and fully present. If you give up, you are guaranteed not to succeed. If you can stick with it, correcting course as necessary, you may be one of the survivors.

3. Review your practice periodically to spot trends and make course corrections.

No practice will ever run on automatic pilot. Steer your practice and change your financial, marketing, or other strategies whenever necessary to stay on course. This means making an operational and goal plan and reviewing it regularly. Monitor whether you are earning as much money as you projected and booking as many cases as you need to meet your goals. If you've been in business for a while and have never done this, there's no time like the present. And always, always make course corrections when necessary, whether they are almost imperceptible or 180-degree turns.

4. Stay fresh.

It's easy to get caught up in success—don't let your practice become a treadmill of success that keeps you trudging from closed deal to closed deal long past the time you run out of energy and enthusiasm for the job. Explore new avenues, shake up the way you do things, talk to mediators who *are* having fun and pick their brains. And if you need a break, take a break.

5. Enjoy the good times!

Many of us tend forget the up part of the ups and downs of the business. When your calendar is booked solid, you're settling every case, and the phone is ringing off the hook, pat yourself on the back and bask in the glory. You're working hard—you deserve it!

8

Looking Ahead

The Future of Mediation and Your Future in Mediation

People go to mediation classes and ask, "How do you recommend I get business?" It's really about so much more than that. You have to choose this profession and make it happen.

Mariam Zadeh

I was in the right place at the right time, and I'm the first to admit it. Still, it's my nature to be optimistic about the future. I know that the way I and my contemporaries did it is not necessarily the way today's mediator must work. The market has matured, laws are changing, and the mediation field itself is more crowded. If you're going to start a mediation career now, you have to approach it in a very different way than we did at the beginning. In this book we have done our best to make clear the many avenues that are open to you as a mediator who aspires to a high-quality, financially successful practice.

Now that we're closing in on the end of the book, we have chosen to look into the future of mediation and to urge you to think about your own future as a mediator. They are, of course, inextricably connected. Ask a top mediator to look in the crystal ball, as we did, and you will get many individual and insightful visions of the future. As you have already seen, we don't always agree. But it is precisely this individuality—and the expansive nature of the mediation profession, which allows for this attitude of playfulness,

Mediation Touches Everyone Involved

I see a brighter future for everyone. When we started, people confused the word *mediation* with meditation or arbitration—they were completely unclear on the concept. Now most people understand generally what a mediator does. The more experience people have in problem solving, the better. The bedrock is communication skills. Effective listening always lightens the tension in every situation. I feel that every successful mediation touches the lives of everyone involved and represents the interconnectedness of all of us. It has a deep spiritual dimension if you look at your work that way.

Jeff Abrams

thoughtfulness, boldness, and experimentation—that has enabled the mediators who participated in this book to climb to the top of the pyramid.

THE FUTURE OF MEDIATION

I have lived through the infancy, childhood, and adolescence of the mediation profession. In many ways, I feel like a proud father who has seen his child successfully launched into adulthood. Still, as every parent knows, your responsibility doesn't stop there. It's up to us as professional mediators to ensure that mediation continues to mature in ways that make us proud. That said, let's look at the trends in the mediation field today. Some are not so hopeful, some are more hopeful. A realistic assessment of where the practice is going is not just an exercise in philosophizing: it can be a practical guide by which you shape your career in the years to come.

Not-So-Hopeful Trends: Institutionalization of the Process

We are now living in a society that has, by and large, accepted mediation as a dispute resolution process, and we are seeing a steady increase in the number of cases going to mediation. This is remarkable and heartening to those who love the profession.

In the last several years, however, mediation has learned to depend on litigation to feed its hunger for business. In the early stages of the mediation movement, the opposite was true. Litigation needed the process of mediation to decongest the court system, presumptively save money for clients, and allow more control of the outcome to the parties. Today, litigation views mediation as a commodity rather than as a useful resource.

"When I got in the field I was spoiled," says Paul Monicatti, "because people willingly and voluntarily came to mediation. Now, with the new mediation court rule, judges are exerting pressure on people to come in to mediation. This changes the dynamics. Because some parties are reluctant or unwilling participants, their minds and hearts simply are not vested in the process. Now I see mediation becoming just another stage in the litigation process." New Zealand's Geoff Sharp also sees this trend. "Many mediators have an unfortunate tendency to be unduly reliant on court systems to feed them cases. I do think that there is a real danger in all jurisdictions of mediation needing litigation more than the other way around."

"This is a big mistake," says Jeff Kichaven. "Court systems will inevitably regulate mediation, but not in ways that are consistent with the values of the mediation profession—originality, creativity, spontaneity. They will regulate in ways that are consistent with the legal system: regularity, predictability, consistency. We are supposed to be *alternative* dispute resolution. If we rely too much on the court system, it will suck the life out of what we do. We have to be willing to rely on ourselves to convene and administer our cases at our own expense. We can't take the easy way out. There's no such thing as a free lunch."

Not surprisingly, lawyers have come to dominate the mediation profession. For some, this is a plus. Ralph Williams says, "My point of view is the point of view of a former trial lawyer, and my clients are trial lawyers. In the lawsuit world, mediation is here to stay, as another tool in the trial lawyer's toolbox. And it will probably get bigger than it is now." For others, the predominance of lawyers is a mixed blessing. "A tremendous number of lawyers are interested in alternative dispute resolution," says Chris Moore. "They bring a lot because of their legal expertise and background, and that's a good thing. When you have a profession as powerful as the legal community that sees mediation as being advantageous, that is very significant. The problem is when they decide they want to capture the field, and limit who can practice to only those who have law degrees or market it in such a way as to say that only lawyers would have the information to be able to practice in that arena, which is not true. Many people in the legal community would very much like to be the primary, if not the exclusive, provider for dispute resolution services. In several states they have actually been successful at limiting some of the practice of mediation to lawyers, or making it very difficult for nonlawyers to get in, especially on cases referred by courts."

As a former trial lawyer who found my dharma in mediation, I can see a number of reasons for lawyers to continue joining the profession! Nonetheless, variety is the spice of life, and the field of mediation is no different. Some of the most effective mediators in the world are nonlawyers. Consider Cliff Hendler, who is considered one of the most creative problem solvers in all of Canada. Cliff did not go to law school, but he has substantial experience in the field of risk management, so he came to the profession with a definitive understanding of the decision-making process. That background, coupled with his colorful personality, makes him a natural as a mediator.

In a sense, the institutionalization of mediation is a "be careful what you wish for" result. In the late 1980s and early 1990s, mediators pushed to add mediation as an item on the menu of legal options that were offered in the civil justice system. That system resisted our efforts for many years, but then realized that not only could it obtain better statistics in terms of closed files but also increase client and attorney satisfaction—at which point mediation became the hottest thing in town. Everybody just had to have it.

Once that occurred, the usual administrative machinery took effect, and regulations were installed. Those regulations included local court rules that mandated the use of mediation at certain points in a case without requiring any analysis as to whether mediation was even appropriate to unlock the dispute.

This idea of mediation as a panacea for all court cases has backfired. The mandatory nature of the process caused lawyers to treat it less as a creative and innovative opportunity and more as a required function along the way toward trial. Mediators then modeled their behavior after what lawyers wanted in the process, and some became professional messengers merely delivering the good news and the bad news in caucus format. For the process to reenergize, the civil justice system would be well served to back off from its mandatory approach to the use of mediation and to let the marketplace be the arbiter of what process makes sense to solve litigated disputes.

Not-So-Hopeful Trends: The "Stale" Mediator

I am a huge proponent of mediation as an improvisational process: thinking on your feet, seeing each mediation as unique, working in the moment, and staying creative seem to me to be the essence of successful mediation. Sadly, along with institutionalization has come a decline in the appreciation of the process and the phenomenon of the stale, "lazy," or uncreative mediator. For mediation to continue to grow, there needs to be a reacceptance of the process and a new shot of creativity into the system.

Due to the proliferation of mediators and the reliance on litigation to feed this animal, mediators are forced to conform their practices in a way that limits development of strategic techniques and creativity. This conformity means that the mediation "product" has become a low-margin commodity in many circles. Mediators copy each other in style and lose their ability to differentiate themselves. Even the high-priced mediators begin to look like their litigation counterparts, basically offering the same service.

Many mediators, including Cliff Hendler, agree with this assessment. "In the beginning," he says, "mediation was novel and creative, and people were intrigued. People would go to mediation with an open mind and listen to creative solutions. Nowadays, people in mature markets like Los Angeles, Miami, and Toronto have 'been there, done that.' Mediation is in danger of becoming too embedded in the litigation field. Lawyers want to regulate what we do, how we do it, and where we do it, and that takes some of the creativity out of it."

Clients can tell instantly when a mediator becomes stale, and the mediator can tell too. In the best-case scenario, these mediators end up seeing the same clients over and over again based purely on the power of their personality. In the worst case, the phone stops ringing.

Even though the most innovative mediators have transformed their practices into unique processes in which they are able to charge for their experience and wisdom, the mediation profession is trending dangerously toward the predictable. Some in the legal profession think they know more about the mediation process than mediators do; the process itself has often become stale, the mediator expendable.

Not-So-Hopeful Trends: Instant Mediators

It has become all too easy to take a forty-hour training, print a stack of business cards, and call yourself a mediator. As I hope we have made clear throughout this book, this is not the road to success—on a personal level or for the profession as a whole.

Lawyers who bring cases to mediators often resent them because lawyers perceive mediating as "easier" than having a client and advocating a position. The legal world often wonders out loud why mediators don't have some professional requirements, such as continuing education, grievance procedures, or other annual requirements to maintain their licenses. So do I.

Other professionals, such as doctors and lawyers, have mandatory continuing education responsibilities. For mediation to be viewed as a profession, mediators ought to adopt similar requirements. Because mediation has its roots in parts of several social sciences, continuing education in such disparate but related areas as neurolinguistic programming, cognitive linguistics, improvisational theater, and decision making seem like a natural extension.

Several years ago, there was a trend toward attempting to create certification programs that would license mediators. Initially, the mediation community resisted, and the trend has subsided. Nevertheless, the possibility of certification or licensure will be brought up again in the future and will have substantial backing by members of the legal community who feel that regulation is critical for those mediators who work on court-related cases. That said, it would be useful for the mediation community to embrace credentialing as a way to define who we are and to express our willingness to be responsible for our own malpractice or negligent acts. From a marketing standpoint, being able to tell potential clients that you are licensed in the field will give you more credibility than simply hanging out a shingle with your name followed by the word "Mediator."

Not-So-Hopeful Trends: Rising Business Costs

The commodification of mediation has also meant that large consumers of our service, particularly insurance companies, want to reduce vendor costs. Because mediators have now fallen into the trap of becoming vendors, insurers are managing the costs of the process in a way that allows them to control the marketplace. Even though, as we have seen, highly successful mediators can command extremely comfortable fees, overall rates are going down.

Meanwhile, as compensation for mediators has dropped, the cost of being in business has increased. The reason for this is that large

An Ingrained Process

The future of mediation is solid as an ingrained process, in terms of value to clients. It's not a passing fancy. I believe that in the future, it will be used as the main method of dispute resolution, and litigation will *really* be the last result. In ten years, virtually no case will go to court without first having been mediated.

Cliff Hendler

insurance companies continue to cut costs, yet require mediators to provide more value—large conference facilities, espresso, high-end donuts, lunch menus. In fact, many insurance companies now require mediation providers to supply computerized statistical case information that they can combine with their usual claims analysis.

The result? Individual mediators who actually started the movement years ago are now moving in droves to serve as panel members with various providers, who handle the increasingly complicated business end of the practice. In my opinion, this has resulted in the further commodification of the mediator in that, although there are always superstars, it can be very difficult for clients to differentiate between panel members.

Hopeful Trends: Institutionalization of the Process

Somewhat ironically, perhaps the least hopeful trend is also one of the most hopeful trends for mediation. "There's no question that mediation has grown dramatically over the last fifteen years," says Chris Moore. "What's interesting is the diversity of application. People are trying it out to resolve all kinds of disputes."

"Mediation is now firmly implanted in the legal communities and in corporations as a way to manage costs and minimize risk," says Cliff Hendler. "That people are now using mediation in situations where face-to-face negotiation used to be the main form of settlement proves this." Even Robert Benjamin, who laments the declining creativity of the field, sees this trend in a positive light: "Over the last twenty-five years, we have seen a worldwide effort to institutionalize the notion of managing conflicts through mediated negotiation processes, and to institutionalize that in the codes and, to some extent, the legal cultures of many different countries. From a historical perspective, this is remarkable."

The good news is that almost every law school has now integrated some form of mediation into its curriculum. Indeed, ADR has appeared on the bar exams of many states, and many schools have developed institutes that study dispute resolution throughout the world. In short, the field has matured. It has begun to define itself and discover what the best practices of a mediator are. In that this approach resembles that of many of the other professions, it provides credibility, which is a hopeful trend.

Hopeful Trends: Mentoring

The increase in mentoring, as we have seen, is another very hopeful trend. Again, this draws from the professions in a powerful and proven way. When young lawyers begin working at a law firm, they learn their trade by working with more experienced lawyers. When young doctors begin their professional career, they intern at a hospital for a couple of years and receive training from seasoned specialists. Social workers and therapists are required to put in many hours of internships before they can launch their professional practice. Yet when new mediators start their career, they can simply hang out a shingle and wait for the phone to ring. What's wrong with this picture? I believe that it would be useful, and is even imperative, to model our professional careers after the professions that have preceded us. Developing a mentoring approach that brings new people into the fold is crucial.

Continuing to Grow the Profession

Right now, most mediators have gray hair and no hair. There needs to be a methodology of getting young people into the profession. Co-mediating, associate mediating, starting with smaller cases: How can we bring new people into the fold? Sometimes it's natural—a judge retires, and he's also a good mediator. People just coming out of law school are probably not looking at the opportunity to mediate.

The question of how to continue to grow the profession is a responsibility mediators have to the profession. The young have a responsibility to do it ethically, to be involved with seasoned mediators in a way that respects the process.

First, we need to bring new people in without having to be competitive. New good mediators are good for the profession. The more good mediators there are, the more mediation will be an attraction for others.

Second, let us not be so competitive that we try to undercut each other on our fees. We ought to compete based on the good work we do, not on the price we charge. In the world of the marketplace, frequency of mediations is driven by success, not by price. There are areas of the country that are so competitive that the market becomes price driven, and that hurts everybody.

Let us secure our days, come up with a reasonable fee, and do good work.

Rod Max

The challenge for most mediators is avoiding the fear that the mentee will take their clients. That is a personal challenge that seasoned mediators need to overcome. My associate, Mariam Zadeh, feels that "If you choose not to take on an apprentice out of fear that he or she will become your competitor, the field will suffer. We should want to contribute to the field, and we should find people who we think have potential and are qualified, and impart some of our experience to them."

If you think that it would be just too much trouble or too dangerous, competitively speaking, to take on this sort of "apprentice," think again. On an emotional, mental, and spiritual level, mentoring can be a valuable personal growth experience. On a more practical level, the mentor-mentee relationship is a two-way street, and business moves in both lanes. Being a mentor can actually improve your business and your bottom line. In fact, a mediator who takes on this challenge today is often viewed in the marketplace as someone who has the confidence to give of themselves without concern for losing business opportunities. The fact is, there's a lot of conflict out there and plenty of business, and as mentor you receive a percentage of your mentee's fees. Not only that, but you can actually create *new* business opportunities. Just as money you invest in a savings plan compounds in value, new opportunities compound because of good "press" and increased exposure to others, and through market segmentation.

If you're a successful mediator, think about imparting some of your hard-earned wisdom to the next generation of mediators. If you're just coming up, think seriously about the value of finding a mentor.

Hopeful Trends: Partnering Across Borders

Globalization is a buzzword that attracts a lot of opinions on both sides. But inarguably the increasing influence of the Internet and the "flattening" of the world we are hearing so much about have brought another hopeful trend: more partnering opportunities for mediators across national borders. A mediator in London, for example, may ask a colleague from the United States to assist in a large business dispute so as to give the parties a crosscultural perspective as they begin the process of decision making. Or disputes involving speakers of different languages might require drawing in mediators from around the world who understand the process of facilitation and might be able to communicate better with the current mediator's clients.

Rick Weiler feels that in the future, "Mediation will increasingly be used to resolve transnational commercial disputes. It has a role to play in the furtherance of international trade and globalization. The United Nations has adopted a model law on international mediation in recognition that mediation will have an increasing role to play in the future, more so than arbitration. England, Belgium, New Zealand, Australia, Bosnia-Herzegovina, various African countries, South America, the Caribbean . . . mediation has continued to grow internationally as familiarity with its effectiveness has spread. The strength of the process is that it can help build trust, resolve disputes sooner rather than later, and reduce costs for everyone involved. International businesses and their advisers will increasingly want to be using this process."

Chris Moore sees a hopeful future for mediation and dispute resolution internationally. "Mediation helps people settle disputes in a way that is often more amicable than other alternative processes and helps build customized agreements," he says. "It builds integrative decisions with broad levels of support. It's not that you don't need leaders or decision makers, but historically cultures have relied more on command decisions than on building collaborative decisions through cooperative processes. As democratic values expand globally, you need to have more structures that help people make collaborative decisions."

The world has flattened, according to futurist Thomas Friedman. From a marketing standpoint, there's nothing restraining us from inviting international colleagues to co-mediate cases. Bringing our

The Future Is Proactive

Industry-wide, the trend has been to go from litigation to arbitration, and now the vast majority of work is in mediation. But as great as mediation is, it's still reactive. I believe that the future of ADR will be proactive. This trend is reflected in mediators' expansion and specialization. We see mediators today who are facilitators, conciliators, and mediation consultants. We see more and more corporations using those proactive forms of communication and negotiation. They still use mediation and arbitration reactively, but I think consumers will have a preference for more proactive work as time goes on.

Right now, we do see better use of mixes of processes. In hierarchical environments—hospitals, hospitality, construction projects, film studios—we see a much better use of processes in different situations. For example, corporations used to simply arbitrate all issues. Then they learned to mediate. Now they have learned to use us intelligently. For example, a hotel might decide to settle a dispute with a linen supply company by a quick and efficient arbitration. There are a lot of linen supply companies out there, so this particular relationship is replaceable. But the company might choose to mediate situations where long-term relationships are crucial: employer-employee disputes, interdepartmental conflicts, and so on.

Overall, we see a better use of process by corporations and governments when there is a lot at stake. We've really come along way over the last thirty years.

Natalie Armstrong

practices into the digital era allows us to communicate through video and Internet protocols quickly and effectively anywhere in the world. Mediators are no longer limited by geographical boundaries. For example, if we are handling a case in California and have to wake up a decision maker in London to respond in a last-minute effort at settlement, we can do it.

Hopeful Trends: Public Policy and the Nonprofit Service Sector

CDR Associates, the firm in which Chris Moore and Bernie Mayer are partners, has applied collaborative decision making to a number of public policy matters, including disputes regarding transportation, land use, water, and hazardous waste. Moore believes that these arenas are growth areas for the future. "People want to go into mediation practice fields where their business can be economically viable. Public policy is one of those—the issues are big, lots of people are involved, the social questions are important, and clients have funds to support collaborative processes. But it's one of the harder areas to break into because it is complex, and if people have a problem to solve they go for intermediaries who have experience. Still, new people can break in with local planning departments and local municipalities, to build up their track record."

Natalie Armstrong, director of the Institute for Conflict Management and president of Golden Media in Santa Monica, California, says, "Policy changes are moving toward an intelligent, proactive use of a proactive process. In the EU, for example, we see chambers of commerce utilizing mandatory proactive communication, negotiation, and mediation where it's necessary. They have learned from U.S. mistakes and successes, and have chosen only to replicate the successful movements. In the United States, I believe we will continue to see more and more intelligent use of neutral services."

Mediating in the area of public policy might not be as financially lucrative as mediating the litigated case, but it may be more important in the global realm for its contributions to society, helping solve disputes between warring factions in Afghanistan, working with various constituencies to divide up water rights along the Colorado River, or helping Native Americans figure out how best to work with the federal government. These kinds of issues require intense communication and facilitation abilities and are critical to the success of society. The mediators who do this type of work deserve more recognition than they currently receive. Many people go into the mediation field motivated by high ideals; few stay the course.

Hopeful Trends: Dispute Resolution as a Choice, Not an "Alternative"

"I think the mistake is to focus on mediation per se," says Bernie Mayer. "Our field should be the field of conflict; the question we should ask is, how can we engage ourselves in professionally viable roles that are helping us engage in conflict?"

Chris Moore agrees. "How do you frame making a living as a *dispute resolver* rather than just as a mediator? Dispute resolvers mediate and facilitate. They do situation assessments (not just present strengths or weaknesses of parties' cases, but identify issues and processes for working them through as disputes). Dispute resolvers also teach in universities or conduct independent training programs. Many people have put together an interesting practice that is a combination of things. CDR does all of these. For us it's a good combination because each area of practice—situation assessments, conflict analysis, strategy design, coaching, training, facilitation and mediation, dispute resolution systems design—feeds and nurtures the others. To teach you have to think, and thinking makes you a better intermediary or mediator."

There is clearly a trend in law schools today to develop programs in the field of dispute resolution. I believe that the content of such programs must be integrated into the bar examination. Once that occurs, every law school will be teaching courses in negotiation and mediation. The new generation of lawyers will view dispute resolution as less of an alternative and more of a choice among many options for resolving conflicts.

A Comprehensive Vision for the Future of Mediation

1. Our judicial system would have a robust voluntary dispute resolution component, which would probably be mediation. Mediation for all kinds of disputes would be available essentially through the judicial system and the private sector.

2. Organizations would have a voluntary dispute resolution process in place, such as early-dispute facilitation or mediation, as part of an overall complement of procedures, as well as arbitration and final decision making, rather than simply ignoring problems or leaping to adversarial procedures and decisions.

3. Public policy dialogues would expand to help our diverse society build greater degrees of consensus around public policy issues, and there would be negotiation of what the significant public policies should be.

4. We would have increased use of regulatory negotiations to develop new rules and procedures around very contentious issues where there are large numbers of stakeholders.

5. Nongovernmental mediators would work with the United States on broader international issues, known as Track II Diplomacy, and there would be an increased use of nongovernmental mediators in Track I formal diplomatic negotiations, or to develop proposals where direct government involvement is not possible or desirable. Clearly, the funding for these efforts would have

to come through government agencies—national or international—or international donors.

6. There would be growth in collaborative decision making or dispute systems design, which helps organizations put together these voluntary decision-making components.

Chris Moore

ENVISIONING THE FUTURE

In order to compete in the maturing world of professional mediation, we must outpace the learning curve of the markets we service. That curve involves the increasing sophistication of our clients' abilities to understand and utilize the various dispute resolution options that have become available. One way to do this is for mediators to go back to their roots of collaboration. Like the expert trial lawyer who with increased experience and education gets better at cross-examining witnesses, the expert mediator can begin to collaborate with his or her colleagues to learn new techniques that serve the profession. With today's technology at our fingertips, we could easily set up chat rooms to share techniques. Networking with colleagues through Internet listservs and blogs helps bring together new techniques and strategies that we can incorporate in cases. This is something the International Academy of Mediators has been doing for years.

Co-mediation is another exciting challenge for the future. Imagine a multiparty construction defect case in which you've got ten different constituencies that need to be addressed concurrently in the course of a mediation session. Wouldn't it be helpful to have a trusted colleague co-mediate that dispute so that the parties never feel isolated and bored? That type of collaboration is critical to our continued success as a profession.

On a more personal level, another way to stay current is to make sure we don't take our cases for granted. Though we are all territorial creatures, our clients will not be loyal forever. We must work to maintain their trust. We can also elevate the requirements of continuing education in order to accentuate our commitment to improving mediation. This would overcome our clients' concerns about dealing with a repetitive, noncreative process. We would, in essence, empower our clients by giving them the process they need.

Although the responsibility for change rests significantly on the mediation community, the litigation community would be well served by learning from past experience as well. Consider the course of court-ordered arbitration since it was conceived in the early 1970s. Initially it was a success for both the courts and the litigants. Cases would resolve following arbitration because lawyers took it seriously. Cases were prepared and presented in a formal manner such that they could be thoroughly evaluated before trial.

As time passed, some lawyers began attending arbitrations without preparing, taking the easy road of asking for a trial *de novo* rather than spending the time getting the case prepared. Statistics on the successful resolution of cases following court-ordered arbitration took a nosedive. In fact, the courts became so fed up with the outcomes of court-ordered arbitrations that they have, for the most part, stopped referring cases into that system. Instead, the courts have preferred to refer the cases to mediation, where the parties can actually have a binding outcome following a successful mediation.

Many of my students who volunteer as court-ordered mediators tell me that lawyers are simply not preparing. They are no longer taking the process seriously. Defendants come into the mediation without an intent to negotiate in good faith, and the cases lock up quickly and are put back into the court system. It would seem that history is repeating itself, in the court system at least. Like the arbitration system before it, the mediation system that has emerged through court-ordered programs has begun to slip into indifference.

Where do we go from here? Both sides need to take responsibility for our state of affairs. Mediators could do a better job being cre-

The Conflict Field Should Be About More Than Mediation

Mediation has always been around and always will be around. The question is how much it will be institutionalized, how much it will be part of a freestanding field of conflict specialists, how much it will be subservient to the legal profession. Right now, I think that's up in the air. If we want conflict to be dealt with differently in this world, we want people to learn to use their very best wisdom. I think that's best served by having a rich and diverse field of conflict specialists, of which lawyers are a part. I think mediation is healthiest when it draws strength from many fields but is seen as a freestanding field within the conflict arena.

We also have something to offer in helping create and conduct systems for organizations and communities to manage conflict, and in serving as allies to disputants. Traditionally, lawyers play an "ally" role, as do coaches, strategists, and advocates of a different kind. I think the field needs to think more broadly than just about mediation and resolution. If people are embroiled in conflict, they are not necessarily interested in resolution. They may be interested in taking the conflict to a deeper level or in expanding its reach. We can help people do this in a constructive way that leaves the potential for resolution open.

The conflict field should not be just about mediation. It should be more than that. Whatever we do on our individual cases, the cumulative effect must be to change the way we handle conflict so that it is less destructive and energy draining for systems and communities.

Bernie Mayer

ative and learning techniques that are less predictable. Litigators could invest in preparation and take the process seriously. Or better yet, we could eliminate the court-ordered system altogether and let the marketplace decide which cases should go to mediation.

Ideally, as a case is filed in court, all parties would select a mediator and select a date far enough out for them to learn what they need to know about the facts of the case before the matter goes to trial. In other words, the court would stop imposing time restrictions on when a case should go to mediation and simply acknowledge that the lawyers, as part of their practice, will voluntarily attempt to mediate before the case goes to trial. This already happens in some communities, such as Toronto, but it has yet to extend across the board.

TRACKING YOUR FUTURE IN MEDIATION

People who are at the beginning of their mediation career often believe that there's an ideal world in which they will be successful beyond their wildest dreams. They can see that wonderful world of wall-to-wall bookings and ever-rising fees way out there on the horizon, and they're sure that if they just keep swimming, sooner or later they'll get there. Even the best-known and most successful mediators are not immune from this kind of thinking. As one of my colleagues recently confided, "I'm going to bill $1.6 million this year. That's a lot of money, and I don't have that many expenses. And I don't feel like I'm there yet. I feel like there's so much more I should be doing!"

I can empathize with this guy, and I'm willing to bet that many of the successful mediators who shared their thoughts in this book can too. But I also know that you will never reach that ideal world, no matter how fast or how far you swim. In fact, sometimes it seems that the more you swim, the farther away it is. In reality, you're never going to be able to swim across that ocean to get there. Even if you hit dry land, you're very likely to say, "This is a nice place, but I need more"—and jump back in the water.

In fact, as any impartial observer could tell them, they've reached the other shore—the one they were swimming toward—but *they don't recognize it*. That's because the goals they set are so impossibly high—I'm going to be the next Tony Piazza!—that they block their view of what's really there.

Set workable, achievable goals and allow yourself to measure your real progress. Know that two lawyers can soon *create* ten clients for you. Swim steadily, with a strong stroke, and keep your eye on that speck of land on the horizon. All along the way, pay attention to where you are. If you find yourself swimming in circles, get back on course. And when you feel the ground beneath your feet, stop swimming, rest a while, and enjoy the amazing, successful, and lucrative career you have created for yourself.

TOP-TIER STRATEGIES

1. **Pay attention to new regulations and trends in mediation.**

   They could affect aspects of the process that you take for granted right now. Read the law journals and participate in dispute resolution trade associations that have their finger on the pulse of the legislation in your area.

2. **Remember that success is a full-time job.**

   If your goal is to be highly successful financially and professionally, you must set your goals high and keep your eye on the ball. Becoming successful and ensuring that success is ongoing is a full-time job in itself—it's work you do in addition to the many hours you spend in actual mediation. No matter what trends and directions the mediation profession follows in the future, two elements must always work in tandem to ensure your success: good mediations and effective self-marketing.

3. Know when you've reached your goal.

If you love mediating, it can be much easier to work non-stop and feel that you still haven't worked enough to stop periodically to assess how far you've come. If your goal seems perennially out of reach, stop and take a good look. You may find that you do indeed have a few more miles to go before you get there; but you may instead find, to your surprise, what those around you have long known: you're already at the top!

The Mediator's Field Guide to a Successful Practice

MIND-SET

View Your Work as a Calling

If you thank your good fortune every day that you are able to practice in this field, you are in the right career. Viewing your work as a calling makes it automatically more than "just a job": it is something you are drawn beyond choice to do, and the satisfaction it provides is enormous. Without this feeling that mediation is what you were born to do, your chances of reaching the top of the field are slim. With it—and with a lot of hard work and perseverance—the sky's the limit.

Begin Thinking of Yourself as a Mediator Now

Even if you are just starting out, reframe your self-concept immediately: *you are a professional mediator.* Let this understanding inform everything you do, and wear only one professional hat. When you do, you'll become more attuned to the small and large conflicts that inevitably crop up in daily life, and you'll find yourself thinking about ways to solve them. You'll replay each step in a mediation afterward, looking at it from all angles and seeing what you might have done differently. You'll seek out training and education to hone your skills. You'll find that the challenge of mediation—finding the key that uniquely unlocks each case—will broaden your mind and abilities and sharpen your problem-solving skills. Living and breathing mediation in this way will solidify your intention and your identity, and align you with your life's work.

Practice Mediation Skills in Your Everyday Life

You don't have to be in the caucus room to practice mediation. Life provides endless sources of conflict and a fertile field in which to hone your skills. Whether you find yourself mediating a fight between your two small children or a misunderstanding between a checkout clerk and a customer, you'll learn something you can use down the line. More important, perhaps, paying attention in this way will reinforce your identity as a mediator.

Be a People Person

Mediation is all about facilitating communication, and that requires the ability to reach out, understand, connect, and care about what happens to a wide variety of people. Being an effective self-marketer of your mediation business also requires you to connect positively with all sorts of people. Effective mediators come in all personality types, from introverts to extroverts and every shade between. But virtually without exception, the most successful are those who reach out to others, enjoy being with old friends and making new friends, and show a genuine interest in the well-being of others. This comes naturally to some mediators; for others it's a learned—but vital— skill. If you're not naturally a people person, do everything you can to learn how to be. Learn to speak in front of groups at a Toastmasters club; practice giving the person you're talking to your undivided—and sincere—attention. Become an expert listener. And practice, practice, practice by immersing yourself in group situations. Then just relax and enjoy the ride.

Embrace Rejection

The road to success is paved with rejection. When clients are choosing between two or three qualified mediators, rejection is inevitable for someone. It will be an ongoing part of your world, no matter how high you go. If you can't learn to love rejection, at least learn to shrug it off as part of the process. Remember all the good things they must have said about you to put your name on the table in the first place!

Stick with Every Case

Nobody ever became successful by giving up. Do whatever it takes for as long as it takes to settle every case. This is an expected and necessary part of negotiation. A reputation for giving up too soon will put you in the "do not select" category and sink your career before it starts. If the timing is not right to finalize a deal at the mediation, your assertive and persistent follow-up—on the phone, by email, in person, and in remediation—will usually settle it. If the case doesn't settle—and a few never will—you, your clients, and the parties will know that you went beyond the call of duty in your efforts to bring them closure.

Embody Trust

Develop a reputation as a person who can be trusted. People who don't trust you won't hire you—it's that simple. The most successful mediators are the ones who inspire others to trust them and who hold that trust sacred. Once you are hired, you must continue to earn clients' trust, even under the worst circumstances, when conflict has made the clients unbearable to be with. Be balanced and fair in your approach, and you will live to mediate another day.

Practice Authenticity

Authenticity is the bedrock on which trust is built. Being authentic requires you to be strong enough to work with ambiguity, day in and day out. This ambiguity sometimes leads to an internal conflict over how to be honest with yourself and others, yet be fair and trustworthy. You can't always know where things are going or how you are going to get there, but you must lead from an honest heart. This will give you the ability to walk the fine line between deception and honesty and to make the parties feel that you always have their best interests at heart.

Practice the Three P's: Patience, Perseverance, and Persistence

Every single mediator who made it to the top did so because he or she understood the importance of patience, perseverance, and persistence. It can take three to five years to build a successful mediation practice, so relax, dig in your heels, and prepare to be there for the long haul. Believe in your abilities, believe that you can and will build a successful career, be sure to back up that assurance with real skill and real successes, and then stay the course.

Invest Time, Capital, and Energy in Your Business

Becoming successful, contrary to rumor, is more than a matter of luck: it requires a tremendous commitment of time, capital, and energy. Mediate well and pour everything you've got into making sure people know you and know you're in business. Your personal investment of time and energy—on a continual basis and always in positive, productive ways—will pay dividends in goodwill, interest, and new business.

Stay the Course

The mediation field is littered with the bodies of mediators who gave up too soon. It takes perseverance to make it to the top of this field, and that means giving everything you do a fighting chance. If you send a thank-you note to a client but you never hear from him or her again, don't assume the thank-you note went unappreciated. Follow that up with a phone call to see how things are going and to ask if there's anything you can do for him or her. If that doesn't pay off immediately in a booking, don't despair. If you continually put your positive energy out there, eventually you will begin to see returns. It's important to remember that your marketing efforts will probably not pay off overnight. If you stay the course, you're more likely to finish in the lead!

Be Creative and Innovative

Mediation is a fertile field for creative thinkers. Be as innovative and persevering in your marketing efforts as you are in your efforts to find the path to settlement for the most complex conflicts. You may dress conservatively for work, but your clients will expect the unexpected from you in settling cases. Demonstrate your brilliance in everything you do.

Stay Fresh to Survive

Everyone gets tired at some point, but you'll survive in this business by making an effort to stay fresh in your approach and your outlook toward your practice. Do all you can to maintain your compassion for the parties. If, despite your best efforts, you find yourself getting stale or robotic in your approach, take corrective measures fast. You can get your blood pumping again by collaborating on ideas with other mediators or taking "educational vacations" to exercise your mind by learning about faraway places and far-out ideas.

Always Express Gratitude

It can't be stressed enough how personal the mediation business is. The same points of etiquette that apply in social life are magnified in the intense emotional arena of a mediation. After a case is over, always show your appreciation to clients and parties with a note or email of thanks to express your gratitude for their participation or professionalism. This is a genuine gesture of appreciation *and* an invaluable marketing activity. Clients will always remember this small but important show of human connection.

GOALS

Define What Success Means to You

You can never reach the Promised Land if you don't know where it is! What does success as a mediator mean to you? Just saying you want to be "successful" is too general a goal to reach. Is success having a career that allows you to pursue your chosen work? Does success mean making a boatload of money? Perhaps for you it means enjoying your work, helping people, earning a substantial living, *and* spending time with your family. Whatever your goals, clearly defining them frees you to focus on achieving them.

Set Achievable Goals and Continually Assess Your Progress

Once you've defined your success goals, set your financial and business goals. Make your goals very concrete. What has to happen in your practice—at every stage of the game—for you to reach your ultimate goals? Assess your progress regularly. You may be surprised to see just how far you've come in a relatively short time.

Create a Personalized Goal Tracker

Make a goal-tracking sheet for your mediation practice. Tracking your goals can be a powerful motivator and can help you identify and avoid obstacles before they appear, encourage you to brainstorm strategies and solutions, and help you pinpoint the intended results of your efforts. Use the goal tracker in Chapter Five as a template.

Create a Financial Road Map

When you're struggling to fill your calendar, it can be difficult to see how you're ever going to make a living as a mediator. Build a realistic picture of how your growing financial success will look by creating a financial road map. Graphing your projected gross revenues over a ten-year period is an effective way to demonstrate to yourself how your income can incrementally increase. This simple chart can help you persevere toward achieving goals that seem unattainable but soon become surprisingly doable. As you would with any projection, return to it periodically and reassess your progress.

Build Marketing Efforts into Your Schedule

Create a schedule of marketing projects you are working on and a time line for completing them. When you have an empty space in your calendar, pull out one of these projects and work on it. Or schedule one day a week on a regular basis to devote to marketing efforts. Mediating all the time may be more enjoyable, but it won't get your name out to the marketplace effectively.

Know When You've Reached the Top

You can keep striving forever, long after you've actually achieved your goal. If you've been too busy to see that you have actually become a successful, in-demand mediator, stop right now and smell the roses. Enjoy your success and be sure to share it with others.

BUSINESS

Make a Business Plan

You can't go wrong starting your business by creating a business plan. This is where you define your business and nail down your goals, set out your financial parameters, and conduct a cash flow analysis. If you are new to the business end, get help from a CPA, financial consultant, or general business consultant. This will help you take your business seriously and ensures a firm foundation from which to proceed.

Don't Quit Your Day Job; Do Quit Your Day Job

Successful mediators say, "If you want to become successful, don't quit your day job!" And then they quickly follow up: "But if you want to be *really* successful, you have to make a full-time commitment." What are they talking about? As we've said elsewhere, it takes three to five years to build a successful mediation practice. At the beginning of your career, especially if you are making a transition from another career, you will need a source of additional income—so don't quit your day job right away! Eventually, however, you must take the plunge and commit to mediation as your full-time career. While you've still got your day job, devote meaningful time and thought to figuring out how you are going to make the transition and meet your financial responsibilities.

Look to Other Mediators as Good Sources of Business

Competitiveness is bad for the mediation business. Most professional mediators are friendly, outgoing people who form long-lasting friendships with their peers. Getting involved in professional mediation organizations can often result in referrals from other mediators who are either overbooked or in geographically challenged locations.

Explore Market Segmentation

If your goal has been to reach the high end of the market and you've achieved it, it may be time to set a new goal. Assess your practice to determine whether it is feasible for you to create opportunities at different levels of the market, such as large complex cases and smaller employment cases. Depending on where you are in your practice, you might consider aligning yourself with someone who handles the segment of the market that you don't handle, and developing a referral relationship between the two of you. This can result in increased business for both of you, a larger client pool, and a new set of contacts; it can also reenergize your interest in your business.

Enjoy the Good Times and Make the Most of the Down Times

Accept it: your practice will have cycles and seasons. The phone will ring off the hook at times and get dusty at others. The key is not to panic but to use your free time wisely. Focus on tasks that will continue to put your name in lights, such as writing a column for a legal journal. Learn to enjoy and use the down times just as you enjoy the busy times.

If Entrepreneuring Is Not for You, Consider Joining a Panel

You need to have a reputation for success before you'll be asked to join a panel, so this is not a decision you can make at the beginning of your career. However, if you find that you're not cut out to be a sole practitioner, joining a panel may be the right career move for you. Panels make your business life easier by providing office space and by handling marketing, scheduling and administrative functions, and billing and collection. On the downside, you run the risk of being perceived as a commodity rather than a name brand. If you do choose a panel, work hard to maintain your uniqueness.

WORKPLACE

Learn to Work Anywhere

It's the rare mediator who has a mediation center and never leaves it. Some mediators are on the move virtually every day. Learn to work effectively wherever you are. With a laptop or PDA, you can catch up on email or write an article while you're waiting for a plane. Make use of long driving times to call clients or catch up on administrative conversations with your staff. If you've had a long day at work, don't stay until 2 A.M. finishing up paperwork. Go home, relax, and finish your to-do list in the comfort of your home office.

Let Your Workplace Reflect Your Personality and Interests

If your mediation center expresses your interests and personality, you'll form an immediate connection with clients. It will be clear that you enjoy being there, and they will enjoy getting to learn about you as a person. Knowing you in this way relaxes parties and allows them to feel more comfortable in opening up about sensitive details of their lives. And for you, it's a comfortable place to work!

Invest in Creature Comforts

Invest in the comfort of your clients and share something of yourself in your caucus and conference rooms. Never underestimate the power of a comfortable chair, a good cup of coffee, and an interesting environment. When you do everything possible to meet clients' needs and help them feel at ease, in terms of both their case and basic creature comforts, they will want to return.

Get Rid of Your Desk

Remember the rule: "No desk, no clutter." Sitting at a desk all day gives you the false impression that you are busy. When you're at work, be at work. If you're not mediating, work on marketing your business or take a deserved day off. You can always set up your laptop on the conference table if you have to send email or write an article. If you really need a desk, keep it at home.

Declutter Your Work Life

A desk isn't the only way to accumulate clutter: you can also clutter up your work life with too many interesting activities—teaching, writing, taking courses, meeting and greeting—that keep you from actually getting cases and closing them, which is the heart of your real work. Look at your activities and eliminate the ones that are getting in your way instead of helping you.

Avoid the Crackberry Syndrome

We tend to love our toys, and being able to stay in touch wherever you are is invaluable. But when your need for communication becomes obsessive and constant, you detract from your professionalism. If you're constantly checking your email or your voicemail during a mediation or client meeting or lunch, you are not present with your clients. People who feel they are not holding your interest will soon find another mediator who will give them undivided attention.

POSITIONING

Don't Claim to Be a Generalist

It makes a certain kind of sense to think that if you put yourself on the market as a mediator who can work on any type of case, you'll have a chance at every case that comes along. In fact, the opposite is true. You can't be all things to all people. If you tell the marketplace that you handle "all" types of mediation, thinking that you'll get "all" types of cases, you're in for a rude awakening. This statement is so general that it's meaningless, and it just dumps you back in the steaming pot of mediators who are climbing on each other's backs to leave the crowded bottom tier.

Know Something About Something

When you are developing a practice, you'll put yourself way ahead if you lead from your strength. Perhaps you have been a lawyer specializing in mass torts or a psychologist with a specialty in bringing together disparate groups of people or an insurance claims agent with an inside knowledge of the insurance industry. Whatever your background, find a way to make it work as a focus for your mediation practice. Why try to break into a substantive field of mediation that you essentially know nothing about when you already have knowledge and contacts in a specialized area? This is no time to reinvent the wheel.

Choose Your Market Niche, Target It, and Stick to It

Once you've chosen your position in the market, market to the group of people most invested in it. For example, if your expertise is in intellectual property, be sure to get the word out to this community that you are available and interested in these cases. Give talks targeted at intellectual property lawyers or software manufacturers and write articles in the appropriate journals. Attend functions of groups interested in intellectual property and get to know the players and their concerns. Soon this will make you the go-to mediator for intellectual property cases in your community.

MARKETING

Mediate Well

The best advertising is not the $2,000 ad you might place in the local legal journal. It's the great work you do with your current clients. Satisfied clients have a strong desire to be your best advocates. Keep them satisfied, and you'll keep them coming back.

Give People a Story to Tell About You

What's the buzz on you? If you're not being talked about in the marketplace, you're just one mediator on very long list. If you give people a great story to tell about you, it will be your most potent marketer. A reputation for closing cases is the best story there is—but somebody has to tell it for you. To make this happen, get involved with your target groups, such as bar association committees, and participate actively. Write articles for selected publications that your constituency reads. When people know you, they'll talk about you. In short, get your name in lights and work hard to keep the lights on.

Understand Supply and Demand, and Make Yourself a Standout

Here's the brutal reality: there are far more mediators than there are mediation opportunities. Think hard about who you are and what makes you unique, and how you can help your clients and potential clients recognize that uniqueness. Find creative, compelling ways to help yourself stand out from the pack. Put your name and face in front of your clients with enough frequency that you become familiar—a known quantity they respect. Whatever you do, be discriminating in the marketing choices you make for your practice.

Cultivate Champions

Mediators, especially sole practitioners, often go it alone in establishing a business. It can be a tremendous boon when successful associates tell your story, recommend your services, and generally promote your career out of friendship and admiration. Do what you can to develop sincere relationships with influential people who believe in what you do and who you are. These are the people who will be your active sales force in the marketplace—sometimes without ever realizing it.

Let Your Props Tell a Story About You

Decorate your workplace with items that have meaning for you; they function as props that give people details for the story they tell about you. You will be the mediator who not only closes cases but also has the hand-carved Native American talking stick or the autographed baseball from the early years of the sport or the fascinating book of rare maps. This kind of marketing is effective and fun, and it takes on a life of its own.

Understand Teaching as a Form of Marketing

Teaching can serve as a great entrée to new clients. Many lawyers who take your course will never go into the field full time, but they are likely to think of their mediation instructor the next time they have a case going to mediation. Another benefit of teaching is the marketing your course does for you: many schools create brochures and ads underscoring the high quality of their instructors, and your name, CV, and photo will be seen by hundreds of people—without your having to lift a finger.

Use Speaking and Writing to Sell Yourself as an Expert

Speaking or writing on any old subject probably won't get you far. But you can develop a reputation as an expert in your particular area of expertise if you become an effective speaker and interesting writer who can make these issues come alive. Bring this effect home by focusing on your target audience: speak to interest groups and publish in journals your clients will read.

Identify the Gatekeepers and Go After Them

If you identify the people who select mediators, you can cultivate them. Parties rarely select mediators, but lawyers have to settle case after case. That's why they are the obvious gatekeepers when it comes to selecting mediators for litigated cases. Government agencies are also gatekeepers for public policy disputes. Sometimes corporate clients keep track of who they like to use for mediation in various locales. Once you've identified them, go where they congregate and make some new friends.

Remember the Butterfly Effect

You never know how large an effect your smallest effort will have. Don't think you have to go for the big score every time—a talk you give at a brown bag luncheon may impress a listener with your expertise. That one listener tells a friend about you, who in turn tells a friend who is looking for a mediator who understands just this subject—and you may land the case that proves to be your tipping point. This is not an effect you can try to control—that's just about impossible. It *is* possible, however, to be aware of the butterfly effect and ensure that all your efforts and interactions are as positive as possible.

Fish Where the Fish Are

It's pointless to put your efforts into impressing groups that will never use your services. It's good to attend functions, but it's a waste of time if your potential clients aren't also in attendance. Always target your talks, articles, and other marketing efforts to people and groups that share an interest in your chosen niche. Socialize with the people you want to do business with—and have fun doing it!

Be the Last Person They Speak To

The last person someone speaks to is the first person he or she thinks of. Check in regularly with clients and potential clients to see how a case is going or just to ask if there's anything you can do for them. Keep your name in front of them by writing articles for journals they read or speaking to groups they attend. The next time they're looking for a mediator, you just may be the first person on their mind.

Continually Update Your Database

Whenever you meet new people, ask if it would be all right to add them to your database—and, if you have an email newsletter, to include them on your mailing list. Keep notes on where you met, their

The Mediator's Field Guide to a Successful Practice   213

affiliations, cases you have been involved in together, and how they settled. Use your database as a reference when you make contact calls. Send thank-you notes and cards as appropriate.

Create a Web Site That Invites Personal Contact

Everybody needs a Web site these days—the trick is not to overload people with too much information. Make sure your Web site provides just enough information to entice people to contact you to learn more. Give them the basics—your CV, information about your practice, your picture, articles you've published, testimonials or good press you've received—but make sure to leave them a reason to call. Why? Because ultimately it's the personal connection they make with you—not the bits and bytes about you—that they'll remember when they're looking for a mediator.

Make Sure Your Email Newsletter Is Not Seen as Spam

Nobody needs more spam in their inbox. If you put effort into creating an email newsletter for your database, make sure to ask people if they want to opt in—don't just send out email because you can. Once they've opted in, give them something valuable to look forward to: new information or an innovative tip or technique they can put into practice.

Cater to Different Learning Styles

Some people read the *New York Times* online; others get it delivered to the front door. Everyone takes in information differently. Make sure your marketing covers all the bases—visual, tactile, up close and personal—to respect all learning and information preferences. A personal card in the mail, an email newsletter, a link to your Web site, an article you've recently published, a small ad in a legal journal, your speaking at a luncheon—a combination of approaches will have the best chance of reaching the greatest number of people.

Frequency Trumps Size

Regularly place small ads with your firm name and photo in targeted journals just to serve as a reminder that you are still in business. Don't expect these ads to generate business; their fundamental purpose is to boost name recognition.

Avoid Generic Mass-Market Ads

Generic mass-market ads may seem like a good value, but by splashing your name and face all over the media indiscriminately, you'll really be devaluing your name. No one ever hired a mediator because of a great ad. The only real purpose of an ad is to remind people that you're still in business. Small ads placed frequently but discreetly in the same publication will provide better value.

Be an Interesting and Interactive Speaker

Practice these five basic rules whenever you speak to a group:

1. Make sure that you are the sole speaker. You'll be much more memorable on your own than you would be as one of several talking heads.

2. Control the room. Be in charge in the lecture hall just as you are in a mediation. If you don't control the room, you'll lose your audience very quickly.

3. Discover your listeners' problems and give them solutions. Most people go to a talk hoping to learn something they can use in their own work. Make sure you address the specific concerns of the group you are speaking to.

4. Be interactive. A one-way speech is usually a snoozer. Ask for responses and engage people in dialogue to liven up your presentation.

5. Speak to your listeners' worldview and use their language. Every interest group is almost like a small island nation.

Group members have their own language and customs, and if you don't know them, you'll be perceived as an outsider.

MONEY

Value Your Time and Set Your Fees Accordingly

Setting your fees too low devalues your work and the field as a whole. Setting your fees sky high just because you think you can is unrealistic. Assess your market realistically, then charge what you feel you're worth and stand firm. If you don't put a high value on your skills and your time, who will?

Use a Consistent Fee Scale

It's tempting to use a variety of fee scales based on the complexity of cases, but it can also confuse the marketplace. It's far simpler in terms of billing and client communications to be consistent. Although you might lose market share in some areas, you're likely to gain respect and market share in areas where litigants are not price conscious.

Make Your Financial Practices Clear

Clients don't like surprises unless they are happy surprises. Spend time thinking about your financial practices in regard to your clients: Will they pay for a half day or full day ahead of time, or will you bill them after the mediation for hours spent? Will you charge a cancellation fee, or will you be open to rescheduling at no charge? We all have our preferences, and there's no real "right" way. The important point is to make your practices clear and stick to them.

Keep Overhead Low

Keeping overhead low is key to earning a comfortable living. You do not need to spend a lot of money on office and staff to have an effective mediation practice. Many mediators find that they have no need for a brick-and-mortar workplace of their own because their clients are law firms with their own large conference rooms and offices. Others spend most of their time traveling to clients and working out of town. For most mediators, staffing requirements are also small. It's crucial to have a warm, personal voice answering the phone and convening your cases when you're unavailable, but other than that, most office functions can be contracted on a part-time or as-needed basis.

Invest in Your Staff

The key point is to maintain a low overhead, but that doesn't mean you should scrimp on paying for staff. A terrific convener who answers the phone with a smiling voice and savvy questions can be your best agent. Your investment of time, money, and interest in that person can result in a satisfied employee and will bring in more bookings and more revenue. Be generous with time off and planned vacations.

Choose a Profitable Niche

All mediation practice areas are *not* created equal. If you are drawn to an area that is inherently less profitable, such as community disputes or family mediation, you will have to come to terms with the fact that your ability to earn a substantial living will be limited. You have a very good chance of having a profitable career if you practice in a profitable niche area. Usually this is an area that involves multiple parties or high-value litigated cases. If earning a comfortable living at mediation is part of your goal, follow your interests and expertise to the practice area that combines good fit with good finances.

Be About More Than the Money

Even if your main goal is to be among the highest-paid mediators, never let your practice be solely about the money. Mediation is a personal business, and a practice that always keeps people in the forefront will be the most successful in the long run.

LEARNING

Evolve

Mediation is a dynamic process. The success of every mediation depends to a great degree on your staying aware and alive in the moment and bringing to bear every skill you have. If you're paying attention—not only to your work but to everything you encounter in life—you will always be acquiring new skills that will allow you to evolve in your understanding and keep getting better at what you do. Allow yourself to make mistakes, learn from them, and keep moving forward.

Keep Learning

Make ongoing education and interaction with peers integral parts of your world. Forty hours of basic training in mediation are just the beginning. Continuing education is a lifelong affair. You can learn from reading *and* writing, taking a class *or* teaching a class, listening to other mediators talk about their experiences *and* exchanging your own views. You'll never run out of things to learn.

Find a Mentor

If you are at the beginning of your career and aiming for the top, find a like-minded mediator who is already successful in the field and find a way to learn from him or her. Observing master mediators at work can teach you more in one day than you can ever learn in a six-week course. Getting the direct benefit of their experience and contacts can help you leapfrog ahead of the competition. But don't expect to get something for nothing. Ask what you can do to help them: make follow-up calls for them, help organize case files, help convene multiple-party cases that require a lot of scheduling challenge, take on a case that's too small for them. Offer to give back in whatever way you can for the privilege of observing their mediations and getting the benefit of their experience.

Be a Mentor

If you're already successful, being a mentor can actually make you more successful. Forget about being competitive. He who dies with the most toys just ensures that no one else will get to play with them. Concentrate instead on imparting your hard-earned knowledge, skills, and abilities to a new generation. Taking a bright newcomer under your wing and doing your part to grow the profession toward higher and higher quality can be good for your business and good for your soul.

Stay Current

The only way to stay ahead of the curve is to know where the curve is headed. Keep abreast of new laws and regulations that may influence the business of mediation. Even if you aren't a lawyer, you would be well advised to read law journals, as well as mediation journals and journals that apply to your areas of expertise.

Be Proactive

Mediation is but one tool in the conflict resolution toolbox. The future of the profession may lie in proactive communication designed to head off conflict before it begins. Expand your world by learning more about facilitation, partnering, and other innovative approaches to conflict. And don't stop at the borders of your own country: the future of mediation is worldwide. Start now by partnering with mediators in other countries to learn about transnational disputes, working with other cultures, and issues beyond your own backyard.

CREATING VALUE

Always Strive to Create Value

In mediation, there *is* such a thing as free lunch—the one you give your parties and clients to build goodwill during a long, hard mediation. You can easily enhance your reputation as a great human being *and* a great mediator by not sweating the small stuff. During the negotiation, you can do this by showing the clients how to avoid the land mines and coming up with creative problem solving and deals that actually land them in a better place than they were before mediation. And you can add perceived value by providing lunch, snacks, and special coffee drinks and by not charging for such petty things as minor follow-up calls or reviewing modest briefs.

Offer Value in Your Marketing Efforts

The point of speaking in front of interest groups is to attract new clients to your mediation skills and services. Make every effort not to put them to sleep! No one wants to hear the same old speech, your hour-long sales pitch, or your interpretive reading of a Power-Point presentation. Whenever you give a talk, be sure you are sharing a new and interesting topic. If you write an article, go the extra mile to explore an area more deeply or to share a skill or technique you know others can appreciate and use. This kind of openhearted approach can only bring goodwill back to you.

Give Something Back

If you are doing well, be sure to keep the flow going in both directions. Give something back to your profession by participating in professional organizations, sharing the wealth of your knowledge, and helping other mediators who are just coming up. And it's not merely okay to do a pro bono case from time to time—it's the right thing to do.

Explore Public Policy

Mediating in the realm of public policy—whether it involves communities or nations—may not be as lucrative as mediating litigated cases, but it has significant impact locally, nationally, and globally. This is an area in which creative and passionate mediators can do good work. Even if public policy is not your area of concentration, occasional work in this field can open you up, feed your ideals, and recharge your batteries.

Power Your Practice by Creating Goodwill

Set your fees fairly but aggressively, and pay back by giving back. Your hard work and caring in a mediation, and your consideration for everyone who is touched by your practice—your clients, your coworkers, your support staff—will power your practice with goodwill and burnish your reputation. Concrete expressions of gratitude and going the extra mile can take you a long way.

About the Authors

Jeffrey Krivis began his mediation practice in 1989, when lawyer-mediators in Southern California were rare and litigators had to look outside the state for experienced practitioners. Now, more than sixteen years later and having resolved thousands of disputes—including mass tort, employment, entertainment, business, complex insurance, catastrophic injury, and class action matters—Krivis is recognized not only as a pioneer in the field but also as one of the most respected neutrals in the state.

An adjunct professor at the Straus Institute for Dispute Resolution at Pepperdine University School of Law since 1994, Krivis teaches negotiation and mediation skills to lawyers and judges. His experiences as both a working mediator and academic prompted him to write *Improvisational Negotiation: A Mediator's Stories of Conflict About Love, Money, and Anger—and the Strategies That Resolved Them* (Jossey-Bass, 2006).

Krivis is past president of both the International Academy of Mediators and the Southern California Mediation Association. The *Los Angeles Daily Journal* legal newspaper named him one of the top twenty neutrals in the state, and he has continued to appear since its inception on the "Super Lawyer" list published by *Los Angeles* magazine and *Law & Politics Media*. He is featured in the most recent edition of *Best Lawyers in America*. Krivis received the highest rating (AV) from Martindale-Hubbell, the premier legal directory in the United States.

Naomi Lucks has worked for more than two decades as a publishing professional, writing books and helping many others write theirs (as ghostwriter, collaborator, development editor, and coach). She specializes in working one-on-one with writers, helping them discover the heart of their project and express their vision. Naomi is cofounder of YouCanWrite.com, the Online Reality Check for Nonfiction Writers.

About the Contributors

Jeff and Hesha Abrams, of Abrams Mediation & Negotiation, Inc., in Dallas, Texas, are nationally recognized experts in the field of mediation and mediation training. Having pioneered the use of mediation in Texas since 1986, the Abramses work with lawyers and parties across the country in resolving conflict, creating value-added settlements, and making deals in complex business litigation, intellectual property, securities, bankruptcy, and employment-related matters. They have mediated thousands of cases over the past twenty years.

Tracy L. Allen, based in Southfield, Michigan, is an internationally recognized mediator, arbitrator, and ADR teacher, performing ADR services for the International Chamber of Commerce, Institute for International Mediation and Conflict Resolution, the Instituto Carlo Amore (Italy), and the Straus Institute for Dispute Resolution at Pepperdine University School of Law. She has mediated and arbitrated business and commercial disputes, securities matters, and employment disputes, and successfully facilitated complex family business succession disputes and cases involving environmental contamination, reservation of rights by insurance carrier, alleged theft of assets, and breach of corporate fiduciary duty.

Natalie J. Armstrong has been involved in the ADR industry as both a practitioner and a marketer for more than a decade. She is the president and founder of Golden Media, a marketing company dedicated to promoting and marketing the conflict resolution industry. She is also the author of *The Essential Guide to Marketing Your ADR Practice* and managing director of the Institute for Conflict Management, LLC, which has trained more than twenty-five hundred professionals around the world in mediation and arbitration skills and provides mediators and arbitrators to private, corporate, and government consumers.

Robert D. Benjamin, M.S.W., J.D., has been a practicing mediator since 1979 in all dispute contexts, including employment, workplace, and organizational disputes, education, health care, business and commercial, and family and divorce, and is a Fellow at the Straus Institute for Dispute Resolution at Pepperdine University School of Law. He presents negotiation, mediation, and conflict resolution seminars and training courses nationally and internationally. He is also the author of several publications, numerous articles, and book contributions and is a regular columnist and editor for the online publication Mediate.com.

Alan Brutman began his career in dispute resolution in 1991 with Judicate, Inc., the National Private Court System, at that time the third largest nationwide provider of ADR services. In 1993, he and two other key members from their western regional offices, Var Fox and Rosemarie Chiusano, established Judicate West, based in Orange County, California, which promotes a panel of neutrals for arbitration, mediation, and private judging assignments throughout California and the West. The firm's outstanding reputation for customer service and superior administration has enabled it to enjoy great success in discovering, developing, and retaining talent and building the practices of some of the industry's most recognized and successful neutrals.

Steve Cerveris graduated cum laude from UCLA with a major in communication studies in 1981. He received his law degree in 1984 from Loyola of Los Angeles Law School, where he was a published author and Note & Comment editor of Loyola's *Law Review*. After fifteen years as a trial attorney, he became a full-time neutral in 1999, and since that time has devoted his practice to mediating litigated disputes.

Robert A. Creo, Esq., is in private practice as an arbitrator and mediator in Pittsburgh, Pennsylvania. He has significant experience both as an advocate and a neutral in tort, employment, insurance, commercial, construction, real estate, and other practice areas. He has been retained to serve as settlement counsel by law firms to negotiate complex and large claims on their behalf. Creo has served over four thousand days as a neutral since 1979 in thousands of cases, including hundreds of claims of serious injury, death, complex business transactions, and commercial cases involving multimillion-dollar settlements.

Joe Epstein is a Fellow and board member of the International Academy of Mediators (IAM). He is a past president of the Colorado Trial Lawyers Association and a former member of the board of governors of the Association of Trial Lawyers of America. Epstein has served as adjunct faculty for the University of Denver and as a book reviewer for the IAM. An author of numerous articles on mediation, Epstein works throughout the Rocky Mountain and Southwest region.

Gary Furlong, LL.M., is a principal of Agree, Inc., in Toronto, Canada. He has extensive experience in mediation, mediation training, ADR, organizational facilitation, negotiation, and conflict resolution. Furlong has worked in the areas of commercial, personal injury, construction, shareholder, insurance, wrongful dismissal, real estate, and workplace conflicts, and specializes in intervening in difficult organizational and workplace disputes.

Eric R. Galton, of GCB Mediators, Lakeside Mediation Center, Austin, Texas, is considered by many to be a pioneer and defining force in the field of ADR. Since 1989, he has mediated over 3,450 cases, employing a variety of mediation styles, and consistently maintains a 91 percent settlement rate. Galton mediates disputes ranging from a half day to two weeks in length, in cities all over Texas and elsewhere, involving anywhere from 2 to 125 parties from a broad spectrum of ethnic, socioeconomic, political, and business backgrounds. He mediates disputes in more than seventeen areas of law.

Harry G. Goodheart III is a former trial lawyer who since 1988 has dedicated his professional energy to providing mediation in cases throughout the Southeastern United States. He has mediated more than twenty-eight hundred state, federal, and prelitigation cases involving tort, commercial, construction, community, securities, land use, environmental, probate, professional malpractice, employment, transportation, banking, hospital and health care, appellate, agricultural, class action, law enforcement, and intergovernmental disputes. He specializes in assisting parties and their counsel resolve complex multiparty and difficult-to-resolve civil disputes.

Susan M. Hammer is a leading mediator in the Pacific Northwest. She is named in *The Best Lawyers in America 2005–2006* for dispute resolution and is a Fellow in the International Academy of Mediators. She has served as a mediator since 1989 and has mediated a range of business disputes, employment claims of all kinds, personal injury matters, and environmental, land use, and higher education disputes. She is a member of the Oregon and Washington State Bar Associations.

Cliff Hendler is president of DRS Dispute Resolution Services, one of Canada's largest providers of ADR services. He is past president of the International Academy of Mediators and the current vice chair of the Mediation Section of the American Bar Association. During the past thirteen years, Hendler has been retained as a mediator in more than two thousand cases, specializing in the areas of insurance litigation, medical malpractice, and workplace conflict, as well as sexual abuse matters.

Robert A. Jenks is director of Mediation Arbitration Professional Systems, Inc., in Metairie, Louisiana. He has mediated approximately two thousand cases involving tort, construction, employment, commercial, product liability, medical malpractice, maritime, and franchise law, including complex multiparty, class action, and mass tort matters.

Jeff Kichaven is one of California's premier mediators of litigated cases. An honors graduate of the Harvard Law School (J.D. Cum Laude, 1980) and a Phi Beta Kappa graduate of the University of California at Berkeley (A.B. Economics, 1977), Kichaven has been a full-time mediator since 1996 and handles approximately 150 cases per year in a wide variety of civil litigation contexts. He is past president of the Southern California Mediation Association and coauthor of its groundbreaking amicus brief in *Rojas* v. *Superior Court*.

Michael A. Landrum, J.D., cofounder of AMERICORD Conflict Management Consultants and Burk & Landrum, P.A., in Edina, Minnesota, has mediated more than twenty-five hundred cases throughout the United States. These matters have included domestic and international disputes, have involved claims of up to $22 million, both two party and complex multi-party in diverse subject matter areas, including commercial transactions, construction, employment, securities, and many more.

Bernard Mayer, Ph.D., is a partner at CDR Associates, in Boulder, Colorado. Since the late 1970s, Mayer has worked as a mediator, facilitator, trainer, researcher, and dispute systems designer. He has mediated or facilitated the resolution of labor-management, public policy, ethnic, business, family, community, and intergovernmental conflicts. Mayer is the author of *The Dynamics of Conflict Resolution: A Practitioners Guide* (Jossey-Bass, 2000) and *Beyond Neutrality: Confronting the Crisis in Conflict Resolution* (Jossey-Bass, 2004).

Rodney A. Max, partner in Upchurch Watson White & Max, in Miami, Florida, and Birmingham, Alabama, has been practicing for thirty years in the areas of mediation, arbitration, business litigation, and appellate practice. He is one of the founders of the Alabama Civil Court Mediation Rules, and he has conducted thousands of mediations involving more than fifteen thousand court cases (as he specializes in multiparty and class action mediations as well as complex two-party disputes) in areas including wrongful death, personal injury, breach of contract, fraud and suppression, negligence, employment and discrimination, environmental, antitrust, insurance coverage securities, and more.

Nina Meierding is a national leader in the field of conflict resolution and mediation and has been providing training and mediation services for twenty years. She is a former president of the Academy of Family Mediators and served on the board of the Association of Conflict Resolution and many other mediation and conflict resolution organizations. She is the director and senior mediator at the Mediation Center, in Ventura, California. She has mediated over thirty-five hundred disputes and has trained thousands of individuals in businesses, courts, school districts, agencies, government, medical centers, corporations, and universities, both nationally and internationally.

Paul Monicatti is a full-time professional mediator and arbitrator in Troy, Michigan, with extensive training and experience in all phases of ADR, and has served as a neutral in thousands of tort and commercial disputes since 1978 in virtually all areas of law, totaling over $1 billion in resolved disputes. He has also served by court appointment as a mediator, arbitrator, facilitator, case evaluator, receiver, expert witness, umpire, referee–fact finder, and settlement master in the multibillion-dollar Dow Corning breast implant insurance coverage litigation. He is a frequent speaker and author on various topics concerning ADR and has trained mediators privately as well as for court programs.

Christopher W. Moore, Ph.D., is a partner at CDR Associates, in Boulder, Colorado. He is recognized internationally as a leading theorist, practitioner, and trainer in the field of conflict resolution. He has extensive experience in environmental, organizational, public policy, and interpersonal mediation and is the author of the classic and seminal work in the field, *The Mediation Process* (Jossey-Bass, 2003).

Michelle Obradovic is an experienced mediator in private practice with Wise Resolution, LLC, in Birmingham, Alabama. She is an active Fellow of the International Academy of Mediators, the Association of Conflict Resolution, and the American and Birmingham Bar Associations and is a frequent speaker at professional seminars on advocacy in mediation and mediator skills and ethics. Obradovic is an associate adjunct professor at Samford University, Cumberland School of Law, and is coach of Cumberland's ABA Representation in Mediation National Teams.

Bennett G. Picker is a partner in the Philadelphia law firm of Stradley Ronon Stevens & Young, LLP, where he concentrates his law practice in the area of ADR. He chairs the firm's ten-lawyer ADR Practice Group. Picker has an active ADR practice, serving principally as a mediator and arbitrator in complex business disputes and multiparty actions and also as a counselor in ADR matters. Picker is a Fellow of the American College of Civil Trial Mediators and a Fellow of the International Academy of Mediators.

Rick Russell, B.A., LL.B., is a principal at Agree, Inc., in Toronto, Canada. He has a broad range of experience in dispute resolution, having practiced as a civil litigation lawyer, ombudsman, mediator, facilitator, arbitrator, third-party fact finder, and trainer. Rick has mediated more than two thousand cases since 1988. These include business and commercial, bodily injury, disability and general insurance, workplace and employment, estates, human rights, construction, insolvency, real estate, and land use matters.

Geoff Sharp has been involved in commercial litigation for the past eighteen years both in New Zealand and in Australia, and until the end of 1998 he was a litigation partner with one of New Zealand's largest litigation practices. He has specialized in contract, securities, banking, and commercial property litigation, and in the early 1990s began to develop his own mediation practice, which he eventually left his firm to pursue. He is now a barrister specializing in commercial mediation work.

John R. Van Winkle is recognized nationally as one of the leaders in mediation and ADR. He chaired the American Bar Association's Section of Dispute Resolution and has been a full-time professional mediator and arbitrator since 1994. He is the author of *Mediation: A Path Back for the Lost Lawyer* (American Bar Association, 2004) and *Rules on Alternative Dispute Resolution Annotated* (West Publishing Company, 2005). His practice is focused on mediating complex contract, commercial, and insurance coverage issues.

Richard J. Weiler, LL.B., C.Med., F.I.A.Med., is recognized as one of Canada's foremost commercial mediators. Based in Ottawa, he serves as the chairman of the National ADR Section of the Canadian Bar Association and was named the 2004 recipient of the Ontario Bar Association's ADR Award of Excellence. An adjunct professor at the University of Ottawa Law School, Weiler delivers mediation and conciliation, arbitration, and dispute resolution training and consulting services both domestically and internationally. He has been awarded the designation Chartered Mediator by the ADR

Institute of Canada and is a Fellow of the International Academy of Mediators. He serves on the World Intellectual Property Organization (WIPO) general list of arbitrators and mediators and on a number of other mediation panels nationally and internationally.

Ralph O. Williams III has completed more than thirteen hundred mediations and arbitrations. He specializes in disputes involving insurance policies and coverage, bad faith, personal injury, attorney, accountant, real-estate broker and insurance agent malpractice, employment, real estate and business litigation.

Mariam Zadeh spent the last decade as a trial lawyer handling a variety of litigated disputes in California, New York, and New Jersey. She practiced for both the plaintiff and defense bar in the areas of personal injury, medical malpractice, professional liability, and mass toxic torts. Zadeh has successfully mediated commercial, premises liability, medical malpractice, ERISA, and other tort actions as well as matters pending on appeal. Zadeh is an LL.M. candidate in ADR at the Straus Institute for Dispute Resolution at Pepperdine University School of Law. As part of this program, she trained and co-mediated with Jeffrey Krivis in a wide variety of cases. In September 2005, Zadeh joined Krivis as a full-time mediator specializing in ERISA, employment, personal injury, and commercial matters.

Index

A

Abrams, H., 90

Abrams, J. (Dallas), 82, 84, 93, 94, 97, 113, 158, 178

ADR (alternative dispute resolution), 119–122, 131, 161, 189

ADR Services, 161

Afghanistan, 191

Agree, Inc., 131

Alabama, 24, 35, 142, 144, 147

Allen, T. (Michigan), 30, 71, 78, 119, 169, 170

Allocation, negotiating, 145

Alternatives, 100

American Bar Association, 100

Armstrong, N., 189, 190

Association of Intellectual Property Lawyers, 85

Austin, Texas, 86, 152

Australia, 188

Authenticity, 38–41; operating definition of, 40; practicing, 201–202

Axelrod, R., 99

B

Baton Rouge, Louisiana, 161

Bath & Body Works, 112, 113

Belgium, 188

Benjamin, R., 20, 36, 38–40, 59, 185

BlackBerry, 55, 94, 95, 104, 162

Blink (Gladwell), 54

Book speaking engagements, 85–87; and controlling room, 87; and knowing audience, 85–86

Bosnia-Herzegovina, 188

Boulder, Colorado, 13, 44

Bourgeois, G., 152

Brutman, A., 122, 123, 139

234 Index

Buddhism, 115
Business plan, 205
Butterfly effect, 79–85, 212

C

California, 3–6, 101, 141
Calling, work as, 20, 50, 199.
    See also Mediation: as
    vocation
Canada, 131, 138, 140, 180
CDR Associates (Boulder, Col-
    orado), 13, 16, 44, 110,
    111, 190, 191
Center for Judicial Education
    and Research (CJER), 141
Cerveris, S., 34, 41, 145
Champions, 210
CJER. *See* Center for Judicial
    Education and Research
    (CJER)
CLE programs, 82, 86, 103
Clients: and creating client
    resource, 89; keeping,
    happy, 54
Colorado, 140
Colorado River, 191
Conflict field, 195
Conflict Resolution Quarterly, 100
Connecticut Mediation
    Project, 3
Continuing Legal Education
    (CLE), 20
Crackberry syndrome, 94–95,
    208

Creativity, 41–46, 203
Creature comforts, 207–208
Creo, R. A. (Pittsburgh), 12,
    24, 27, 48, 63, 72, 92, 94,
    96, 99, 104, 109, 122, 124,
    132, 143, 164, 169
Cunningham, B., 152

D

Daily Journal (Los Angeles), 6,
    99
Dallas, Texas, 82
Dell Computers, 142
Desk withdrawal, 126, 208
Dickinson, E., 18
Dispute Resolution magazine,
    100
Dispute Resolution Services, 3
"Does the Flap of a Butterfly's
    Wings in Brazil Set Off a
    Tornado in Texas?" 79
DRS Dispute Resolution
    (Canada), 138
Dylan, B., 128

E

Einstein, A., 96, 124
Elevator talk, 69
Email: and Crackberry syn-
    drome, 94–95; and daily
    quotation, 96; newsletters,
    95–98, 213; wise use of,
    94–98
Emotional overload, 168–174

Employment Retirement Income Security Act (ERISA), 46

England, 188

Entrepreneurship, 116, 206–207

Epstein, J., 149

ERISA. *See* Employment Retirement Income Security Act (ERISA)

European Union, 190

Evolution of Cooperation (Axelrod), 99

F

Falkner, R., 2

Fees, 142–144; setting, 144–149, 215

Field guide to successful practice: and business, 205–207; and creating value, 218–220; and goals, 203–205; and learning, 217–218; and marketing, 209–215; and mind-set, 199–203; and money, 215–216; and positioning, 208–209; and workplace, 207–208

Field of Dreams approach, 13

Financial road map, 165–168, 204

First impressions, 59–62

First Mediation Corporation, 111, 112

Florida, 5, 19, 24, 78, 140

Four R's, 57

Friedman, T., 188

"Full-Time Mediator Is a Rarity in California, A" (*Daily Journal*), 6

Furlong, G. (Toronto), 35, 41, 72, 81, 82, 86, 100, 110, 137, 153, 157

G

Galton, E., 9, 86, 123, 152, 153

Gatekeepers: identifying, 211–212; lawyers as, 60–62; other, 61

Gateway, 142

Gadhafi, M., 40

Gladwell, M., 54, 56

Globalization, 190

Goals, 203–205

Golden, A., 80

Golden Media (Santa Monica, California), 190

Goodheart, H., 18, 19

Goodwill, 220

Gratitude, expressing, 71–73, 203

H

Hammer, S. (Oregon), 20, 35, 41, 50, 87, 145, 160, 163

Hendler, C. (Toronto), 11, 25, 29, 30, 33, 42, 43, 48, 60, 99, 110, 113, 123, 138, 143, 151, 172, 180, 182, 184, 185

236   Index

Hewlett-Packard, 142
Hurricane Katrina, 161

I

IBM, 142
Innovation, 41–46, 203
Institute for Conflict Management, 190
International Academy of Mediators, 193
Internet, 92
iPod, 55

J

Jenks, R. (New Orleans), 10, 11, 57, 72, 77, 81, 103, 110, 161
Judicate West, 122

K

Kichaven, J. (Los Angeles), 61, 90, 97, 103, 114, 116, 130, 148, 173, 179
Kirkpatrick, G., 2
Koufax, S., 62
Krivis, J., 1

L

Lake Austin, 152
Lakeside Mediation (Texas), 123, 152
Landrum, M. (Minnesota), 11, 25, 43, 63, 104, 147, 154, 158, 171

Lawyers: from, to mediator, 37; as gatekeepers, 60–62; and neutrality, 119–121; sharing suite with, 125
Learning, continuous, 217
Libya, 40
London, 41
Lorenz, E., 79
Los Angeles, California, 19, 58, 59, 78, 99, 111, 140, 141, 182
Los Angeles County, 6; Superior Court, 4–5
Los Angeles County Bar Association, 5
Los Angeles Times, 7, 8
Lowry, R., 101

M

MAPS, 110
Market: creating own, 45–46; opening up, 82; segmentation, 112–114, 206; working in profitable, 140–141
Marketing, invisible: and closing deal, 68–69; and creating value, 66–68; and embracing rejection, 70–71; and expressing gratitude, 71–73; and familiarity, 63; and first impressions, 59–62; and giving people story to tell, 54–57; invisible, 53–75; and keep-

ing clients happy, 54; and mediating well, 58; and referring business to other mediators, 69–70; and shared similarities as connections, 62–63; and solving client's problem, 64–66

Marketing, visible, 77–108; and book speaking engagements, 85–87; and creating user-friendly Web site, 90–94; and good marketing curve, 84; and involvement in mediation organizations, 88–90; and seasonal marketing, 79; and sparing use of advertising, 98–99; and teaching as marketing strategy, 101–103; and working butterfly effect, 79–85; and writing for credibility, 100

Mass-market ads, generic, 214

Max, R. A., 24, 55, 58, 137, 138, 144, 163, 165, 168, 186

Mayer, B., 15, 23, 43, 44, 61, 78, 110, 111, 138, 190, 195

"Mediating the Litigated Case" program, 5, 101

Mediation: getting established in, 7–8; getting started in, 3–4; and growing new profession, 4–6; passion for, 80; as personal journey, 50–51;

unique ability for, 15; as vocation, 14–17

Mediation, future of, 178–193; comprehensive vision of, 192–193; envisioning, 193–196; as proactive, 189; tracking, in mediation, 196–197

Mediators: and cultivation of champions, 22–24; and getting to top, 29–30; and hard work, 24–27; and keeping busy, 103–105; from lawyers to, 37; and love of mediation, 19–20; qualities of top-tier, 17–29; referring business to other, 69–70; and trust, 21–22

Meierding, N. (Southern California), 12, 13, 41, 47, 89, 116, 117, 147, 160, 165

"Mel," 48

Memoirs of a Geisha (Golden), 80

Mentoring, 112–115; benefits of, 114–115; and finding mentor, 217; and learning, 218; and market segmentation, 112–114; and mentor relationship, 115

Metairie, Louisiana, 161

Miami, Florida, 182

Michigan, 11

Mind-set, 199–203

Minnesota, 11

Money, making: and choosing profitable niche, 138–140; and creating value for everyone, 153–154; and how fees are set, 144–149; and investing in environment, 151–153; and investing in people, 149–151; and setting fees aggressively, 142–144; and working in profitable market, 140–141

Monicatti, P. (Michigan), 11, 57, 77, 110, 125, 130, 159, 162, 166, 170, 179

Moore, C. (Colorado), 15, 16, 21, 22, 43, 44, 109, 140, 145, 153, 180, 184, 188, 190, 191, 193

N

Native Americans, 191

Nebraska, 140

Neutrality, 119–121

New Orleans, 11

New York State, 140

New York Times, 213

New Zealand, 91, 179, 188

Niche areas, 45, 209; choosing profitable, 138–140, 216

Nonprofit service sector, 190–191

North Carolina, 19

O

Obradovic, M. (Alabama), 35, 50, 79, 95, 98, 103, 117, 130, 142, 147, 151, 152, 159, 166

Ohio, 140

Old Course at St. Andrews, 128

Ontario, 98, 131, 143

Ontario Reports, 99

Oregon, 35

Ottawa, 131

Overhead, 215–216

P

Panel, joining, 121–124

Partnering, 120

Partnership, 131

Patience, 159–162, 202

People, as business, 129–132

People person, 200

Pepperdine University School of Law, 4–6, 50, 101, 141

Perseverance, 159–162, 202

Persistence, 25, 159–162, 202

Philadelphia Bar Association, 77

Philadelphia, Pennsylvania, 120

Piazza, T., 41, 197

Picker, B. (Philadelphia), 14, 77, 78, 80, 162

Pittsburgh, Pennsylvania, 24, 141

Plan, making, 116–119; and goal tracking, 117–119
Positioning, 45, 208–209
Possibility, 18
Practice: and creating financial road map, 165–168; cycles and seasons in, 158–159; and dealing with emotional overload, 168–174; evolution of, 111–112; and long view, 158; and ongoing commitment, 164–165; from partnership to solo, 131; patience, perseverance, and persistence in, 159–162; using slow times in, 162–163; weathering ups and downs of, 157–175
Process, 164
Profession, growing, 186
Professionals in Human Resources Association (PIHRA), 83
Props, 211
Public policy, 190–191, 219

R

Recognition, leaving need for at door, 71
Reder, D., 3
Rejection, embracing, 70–71, 200–201

RIMS. *See* Risk and Insurance Management Society
Risk and Insurance Management Society (RIMS), 83
Rocky Flats Nuclear Weapons facility, 44
Russell, R. (Toronto), 79, 84, 93, 95, 96, 98, 100, 102, 110, 120, 127, 129, 131

S

Santa Monica, California, 190
Schedule, sample, 26–27
Seasonal marketing, 79
Sharp, G. (New Zealand), 13, 56, 60, 61, 69, 148, 170, 179
Southern California, 12
Southern California Mediation Association (SCMA), 4–6
Speaking, 214–215
Staff, 216
Stories, 54–57
Stradley Ronan Law Firm, 120, 121
Strategies, 50–51; for building practice, 133–135; for future, 197–198; invisible marketing, 73–75; for making money, 154–155; for sustaining practice, 173–175; visible marketing, 105–108
Straus Institute for Dispute Resolution, 101

Success, 6–7, 23, 30, 203–204
Supply and demand, 210
Survival skills, 170

T

Teaching, as marketing strategy, 101–103, 211
Ten-year revenue projection chart, 166
Texas, 2, 5, 78, 140
Texas Bar Journal, 152
Tipping point: mediation, 57–59; personal, 56
Toronto, 11, 24, 41, 78, 84, 99, 182
Training: and basic training, 47–48; beyond basic, 48–50; and skill development, 47–50
Trends, 167, 168; and dispute resolution as choice, not alternative, 191–193; and instant mediators, 182–183; and institutionalizing of process, 179–181; and institutionalization of process as hopeful process, 184–185; and mentoring, 185–187; and partnering across borders, 187–190; and rising business costs, 183–184; and stale mediator, 181–182

Treo, 94
Trust, 21–22; building, 35–38; embodying, 201
Turnkey operation, 139

U

United Kingdom, 41
United Nations, 188
University of Pittsburgh: Medical Center, 26; School of Law, 26
Up-times, valuing, 168
Utah, 140

V

Value: adding, as mentee, 167; always striving to create, 218–219; creating, for everyone, 153–154; exploring, in marketplace, 219; giving, 86
Van Winkle, J., 37

W

Waite, T., 40
Wayne, John (movie star), 59
Web site, 90–94; to invite personal contact, 213; as point of sale, 93; and wise use of email, 94–98
Weiler, R. (Toronto), 24, 25, 28, 29, 46, 53, 83, 88, 105, 124, 143, 159, 188

Index 241

Wellington, New Zealand, 13
Western Pennsylvania Council
 of Mediators, 26
Williams, R. (Los Angeles),
 54, 58, 68, 90, 97, 100, 121,
 122, 138, 147, 161, 163,
 169, 180
Willis, T. (London), 41

Word of mouth, 56
Workplace, 124–129
Writing, and credibility, 100, 211

Z

Zadeh, M., 112, 113, 115, 117,
 126, 163–165, 168, 169,
 177, 187